STOP believing the lies
BELIEVE IN YOURSELF

The formula for rescuing your self-belief, esteem, confidence, worth, love and happiness

John Smale

www.emp3books.com

WHO IS THE AUTHOR...and who is he to offer help?

John Smale was a therapist for many, many years. He has a deep understanding of problems, their causes and their treatment. As an author he writes in a way that is easily understood and he includes humour, one of the greatest medicines ever.

John explains straightforward and highly effective methods that take into account the people they help. He describes things in clear-cut ways. Simple is never stupid. Effectiveness is always the goal. He is enthusiastic to explain to people that results are easier to achieve than we are often led to believe.

His short stories and metaphor books are well respected and are set reading for some American Universities because they show how therapeutic value can be gained from adding different viewpoints to problems and their resolution can be conducted in simple, constructive and entertaining ways.

He has also written fictional works that explore the darker sides of life.

ABOUT THIS BOOK

We exist in a world where misinformation, untruths and lies influence our lives. Advertisers tell you that you are not good enough but, buying their products will improve you. Social media bullies delight in their artificial feeling of domination control which actually demonstrates that they are the ones with the problems. No wonder we lose our self-esteem, self-belief and our confidence.

In informing the reader how to counter those attacks on our self-belief, this book does not make empty promises. It shows you how to achieve what you want from a base of self-knowledge and confidence rather than by false claims. It is not about selling you a product, yet another self-help book that fails to deliver. It provides solutions that overcome self-doubt and uncertainty and shows the reader what can and will be achieved.

Spreading doubt is the weapon of a bully often used by the very people who have the greatest self-doubt and they think the remedy is to dominate others. When we doubt ourselves, we can end up holding negative emotions including anger, the need to blame, jealousy, tantrums and relationship problems.

You will discover how to gain self-belief based on knowing the difference between the strengths of your own thinking and what you are told to believe by outsiders. It shows how to gain the confidence needed to know, and accept, the knowledge we have about ourselves unstained by others.

Find the keys that unlock the barriers in your mind. Take this chance to change your life. Find how to use your powers of will, suggestion, persuasion to positively influence your health, wealth and happiness.

This book is an amalgamation and rewriting of some of John Smale's previous books, plus much new information.

Published in August 2019 by
emp3books, Norwood House, Elvetham Road,
Fleet, GU51 4HL, England
©John Smale 2019

ISNB: 978-1-910734-31-5

This book combines extracts from
ISBNs, 9781910734209 and 9780955073625

www.emp3books.com

CONTENTS

1

HOW SELF-BELIEF IS LOST

This book is titled Stop Believing the Lies, Believe in Yourself, but it is a different use of the word *'belief'* that sits at the whole centre of success. Belief is an ambiguous word that needs explaining because it is full of traps and uncertainty that we develop from our early days of life.

SO, WHO LIES TO US?
Everybody, including ourselves when the inner dialogue we use says that we are a failure or are damaged. Some lies are innocently told to us, usually to protect feelings. They are referred to as 'white lies'. However, there are other untruths that are told to make us stop believing in ourselves and to let others profit financially, physically or emotionally. When we start to accept the lies told to us as the truth, they mess us up and make us feel less confident in ourselves. We will prevail with the help in this book.

COMPLIANCE AND CONFORMITY SPREAD LIES
From childhood we are taught, persuaded and conditioned to believe in things that do not exist. And this disappointment and lack of belief extends into our adult lives to the extent that the truth we know about ourselves is distorted into incredibility and a lack of faith in our own personal qualities.

We are rarely encouraged to trust in the most important thing for us as individuals, self-belief and our knowledge of our ability to succeed and achieve.

We have been conditioned to accept segregation based on the way life is. There is a hidden set of rules that we are expected to abide by that control our lives from birth. In my past years, grammar schools were for future bosses and scientists. Public schools were for the elite, the future ruling class of rich and privileged folk. Secondary schools were just that, second class education and training for workers and labourers. Minds were set at 11 years old and the direction for lives was prescribed. Some broke the 'rules' and went on to become successful because they believed in themselves and their abilities to ignore the falsehoods handed out at a young age.

There is a subtle but major difference between believing and knowing. Sometimes belief is hope whereas knowledge is learnt wisdom. It derives from setting logical expectations from proof and is based in positive thinking. Knowing is a logical thing that looks for verification. True self-belief comes from inside ourselves. Imposed belief is an emotional hope that becomes a control from outside influence.

We grow to realise that life is full of lies. Father Christmas exists until we learn the truth. Then there are conditional beliefs, 'if you do this, then that will happen.' When it doesn't, then we lose our belief in outcomes based on external influences that want to change our behaviour, usually for their benefit. Think of advertising. The messages appear to create a need that we did not have and are, in fact, about profit for manufactures, advisors and marketing companies that are the real needs.

Of course, stories about Father Xmas, fables, the supernatural and magical things are generally harmless. Metaphors, including fairy tales, can help children to be aware of some of the dangerous things in our lives. The bad wolf in the woods warns children about wandering off into potentially dangerous situations. However, some beliefs are for profit from adults and worse still, manipulation of children.

False information is pushed into us about how our lives can be made better if we believe in the unbelievable: In this range the following can be recognised.

- Horoscopes that have no message other than, 'it is bad now but it might get better. Buy a full horoscope to see your future.' What they feed on is a need to know based on our emotional vulnerability. The lie is that they cannot tell the future. If they could, then wars, assassinations and tragedies could be prevented.
- Politicians tell you how bad things are and how they will improve your life if you vote for them.
- Then there are magical pills and treatments that do not work (excepting placebos). And do you need to use lip, hip and buttock fillers? You were born perfect and the blown-up people who use such things look awful to normal folk.
- Get rich schemes seem to only work for the people who sell them. When lotteries started there were schemes sold to predict the winning numbers. Only by using a time machine could you do that.
- Cults that offer immortal life for the price of being abused, losing your individuality or, ironically, by killing yourself. They give a sense of power to the leaders at the expense of the followers.
- Faith healing. There is good research that proposes that placebos work and therefore, perhaps faith healing could work. In this way, my take would be that if emotional suggestion is

3

powerful enough to promote change then what follows in this book will work, but in a more rational way. Faith healing is based on the power of an individual, with the help of spiritual forces if the unwell person is convinced! Sick people are better off with traditional methods of treatment.

- Spiritualists. Some may help but by giving fake news that will comfort those who have lost relatives or friends. Whether that is good or bad is for personal choice. Remember, much of what happens is based on cold-reading tricks.

- Fake news. Usually to change minds of others. It is another form of manipulation of our emotional thinking. Used by people who have power and want change or by those who have none but want it. And it has been used to manipulate minds about major issues within politics and, for example, climate change being a myth.

To summarise, all create fictitious beliefs in external powers that erode internal certainty.

And there is mental and physical abuse by religious figures telling children absolute lies about how they will be punished in eternity if they do not do what they are told, and if they tell what they are made to do. I treated many people who had been abused by the very people they should have able to trust.

To be positive now, the purpose of this book is to allow you to celebrate your uniqueness. Every zebra has a different pattern of stripes. None are right and none are wrong. They are all beautiful.

Passive belief is hoping, wishing and waiting for something to happen. Results are incredibly rare.

Active belief is knowing what you have to do and knowing that you are able to make those changes. This is the only way and you will find how to do that in the words that follow as you progress through this book.

Some obstacles are small and can be stepped over easily. Some are huge and need to be walked around, climbed over or blown up. Yet, a lot of our obstacles are placed in front of us by ourselves because we have been misled in the way we think about ourselves as humans in society. Those barriers are about to be eliminated by the words you will discover as you continue to read and find your way forward.

As humans, there are two things that we can believe about ourselves. The correct point of view, or an imposed opinion from others.

The wrong ideas come from the seeds planted thoughtlessly by those who have a self-assumed authority and knowledge. These will include misguided parents, siblings, our peer groups, school teachers, bosses, church officials, social media, mainstream media and so on. The list is a long one. But within that list you will find those who made you believe you are not good enough. (Who said I cannot start a sentence with the word, but, for example?)

Overtly or subtlety, we are being told we are not good enough and that becomes dangerous when we start to believe that is true.

The word 'too' is a killer when used for destructive comparisons by others and ourselves. For example, physically you are too tall, too short, too fat, too thin. Your breasts are too big or too small if you are female. And your penis is too small if you are a man. (The porn industry has a lot to answer for in terms of creating false beliefs for men and women.) You are too ugly. You are not beautiful or handsome enough to attract a good-looking partner. Shall I go on?

In material terms you are judged by the size of your car, house, bank balance, job status, where you take your holidays and so on and on.

Comparisons make others feel better at our expense. What expense? Our self-belief. The question to ask is why do others need to make judgements? Is it to artificially build their vanity? Self-belief is truth, vanity is a sign in others that they lack confidence in themselves and they indulge in self-deception and misdirecting others rather than accepting and changing their own realities.

Within this massive inventory of self-held negatives in your life that you have been persuaded to take into your very existence the fact remains that you actually are better than all of that bullshit smeared on you by people who are probably bullies or jealous of the real qualities that you possess. Or those soulless companies that want to take your money for false promises. You are the King or Queen of your life by right.

Profit is the goal. Either emotionally or financially by selling you something to make you seem better. To do that they need to convince you that you are not good enough as you are.

If you buy product X then you will become:
More beautiful.

More desirable.
Better off.
More secure.
More successful.

And there are people who want to profit from putting others down and throwing negatives around to make themselves feel better. The boss who fears your talent in regard to their own job. And people who have authority and who use threats to get what they want from you. They abuse their employees, voters, congregations, partners and whoever they need to extract a boost to their feeling of power from.

There is a pyramid of power which people try to climb to give themselves dominance over others. It seems to be an innate part of nature and extends with a formidable strength into humans. This exceeds the battles for mates with other creatures. The fight for individuals is to the financial, or self-esteem, death. Dictators through history have built their power base protected by henchmen who also benefit from being protected.

Superstitions are a control tool used to damage our self-belief. Karma will repay you for doing something inappropriate for others. The same goes for 'fate'. And there are damaging curses that, if you believe they work, can wreak havoc in your life. It is all hokum, fake news. Misdirection that has power at one end and submission at the other. The Mayans, thousands of years ago, would sacrifice people in the belief their harvests would be improved. There is no proof that it worked to help them other than reducing the number of people who needed food.

That inborn urge to hurt others shows itself in many ways and if you have mislaid your self-belief then you may have been an innocent victim of those oppressors of your life. They should not win. You are like a diamond that has been covered in the faecal droppings of those who have nothing better to offer. When it is washed off, the real you sparkles through.

So, how do I clean up the crap that has been flung at me and how can I start to believe in myself in a positive way?

Ahead of the answers being given, first of all, the need to review the damage is necessary before we carry out the repairs.

Society is another pyramid. The higher up you are the better you think you are seen and feel. The downside is that others get jealous and want you to slip down in the ranks so they can stand on your shoulders and feel higher up themselves. The weapons they use are words and feelings. Self-belief is the shield we will use to divert the attacks, whether they are fierce or subtle.

The pyramids and the hierarchies that people build are there to offer them the power to undermine others to keep their place. When you change the way you think about yourself, they count for nothing. YOU are the best.

I will avoid insulting you by setting tasks and exercises but you may wish to consider those untruths and lies you have absorbed about yourself over time before we move on.

2
CHANGING YOUR THINKING

Determination is a power that can be summoned when you need help. It is a resource for your benefit and well-being when used correctly, but beware! It can be a malevolent force if abused or if it is asked to do something that is impossible.

An effective way to demonstrate how our thinking can be changed is the use of metaphors. They enable us to stand outside ourselves and look in. Metaphors provide platforms for 'thinking outside the box'. To escape mental straightjackets, it is good to discover what they are made from and therefore how to undo the stitching that holds them on.

A suitable example is that of our own personal thoughts as if they were physical entities that can oppose each other. Imagine they fight each other in order to help or hinder. Call them angels or devils, good or bad luck, positives and negatives if you wish but those two sides of your mental coin can make or break your life.

This following shows the difference between the two and how to use positive determination to build, and how to ignore the destroyer of dreams.

The quick explanation is that there is a part of us that will follow logic and another part that is easily influenced by emotion. We have to acknowledge them in our minds and use their resources to obtain our targets whether emotional or material.

What and What are our Metaphorical Foes and Enemies?

Our thoughts should be considered as inner mental resources. For ease of explanation of how to get rid of negatives and promote our inner belief, we have to play the game where we feel they live in your mind rather than in a genie's lamp.

So, your inner supporter is the power that you can summon when you need help. It is there for your benefit and well-being when used correctly, but again, beware because it can be a bad influence if abused or if it is asked to do something that has dark motives it. Basically, it is about your inner dialogue: your thinking.

It will fend off your detractors whether inner or external.

Magic is Illusion and Misdirection

Magic is power beyond what we think is possible. We are made to believe in something by persuasion. Our minds are made to think something that is implausible is actually real. The question is "How did the magician do that?" The answer is the same method your detractors and critics used. They misled you in order to demonstrate their own need for control. They want and wanted you feel that they have something more than you do.

We can easily ruin our dreams when we allow ourselves to be misinformed and misdirected. Yet, the techniques for achievement are straightforward.

We have been influenced by suggestion about what exists and what is possible, probably going back to when we were children. That misdirection is obvious when we know what has been done. Once you know how a magic trick works, it is no longer a mystery. The magic that we need is within our thoughts. All we have to learn is how to summon our fantastic resources for the changes that we need.

Communicating with your Mind.

Ironically, the best way to communicate with your mind is to stop talking to it **until** you have learnt its language.

You talk to it every day, and in negative terms from time to time. It will do as you ask, so if you tell it that you are a failure, you are ugly or that you are unable to do something then never be surprised if those requests are followed.

Blame

Blame is a get out of trouble tactic for some. You might feel blamed by others. Punishing others never remedies your situation, it just shows that you need to learn how to handle the ups and downs in your life by avoiding becoming a bully.

You might want to blame others for your actions rather than correcting them by taking action to prevent future problems arising. Blaming yourself stops nothing. We need to learn from errors and improve. Blaming circumstances should be addressed by changing and improving your state of affairs.

Your mind never evaluates, it spontaneously obeys your commands. If those orders are counter to your wellbeing, then never blame your thoughts, just your choice of words for your wishes.

As logic can never be emotional then the opposite applies. Emotion is never logical. Explain love in rational terms.

Impossible. Our dreams and desires are always emotional but we seem to have a need to explain them in concrete terms. These are the wrong words to use.

The most important language to learn is that of emotional influence rather than logic. This takes us back to magic. Our logic tells us that the outcome is impossible, so the methods used are skilful and hidden from us, but our minds want to suspend that belief to allow the emotions of surprise and awe to pleasure us.

The key element of your mind is emotion.
The stage magician's art is very much in creating an expectation in the audience's minds. It is like the Emperor's New Clothes where the viewers' imaginations created a mass illusion of belief. The Emperor was conned into believing that the suit he wore was made of a fabric that could only be seen by trustworthy folk. He was told that the cloth was invisible to those who were stupid or useless. He was, of course, naked. How many lied about not being able to see the suit, but more importantly, how many people believed that they could see it?

This is the point. Did the people who could not see the suit know the difference between having proof that they must be stupid and would have acted that way for evermore? Did the people who knew they were clever see through the con and kept quiet for fear of what others might think of them? The negative conspirator in your head is like the Emperor who creates an illusion of your stupidity. The positive champion is the one who sees the truth and confirms self-belief.

Later, you will be shown what to say to your mind; so that

positive things happen rather than negative outcomes occur.

Another key element is imagination. Before we embark on talking to this great inner resource, we need to establish how powerful it can be and how we should be careful in our treatment of our minds and desires.

The thoughts you have in your head are a mixture of good and bad. When you say something bad about yourself then that wish will come true. I am ugly, or I am useless becomes an instruction that recalls the false destructive comments you have received in the past and they will do their best to make those negative attributes become your reality. The self-critical part of you will take those words and work their magic with them to make them real in your perception of yourself.

When you tell yourself that you are good looking or that you are worthwhile then the supportive part of you will nod its head and agree but will do nothing to reinforce that belief unless asked properly.

Whilst never treating your benevolent mind as a slave you can treat the bad part as an oaf, an equivalent of a school bully or bad boss who makes mischief for attention.

So treat your own knowledge as your personal guru, the wise person who should be respected. Imagine, for a moment, telling your bank manager to make you a cup of coffee before asking for a loan; or telling your teacher at school to do your project work. You do treat, and have treated, those people that can help you with a sense of distinction. You may not feel it for a bank manager but you pretend it. Your mind is a true ally that helps you for mutual benefit.

Nothing will reward you for being a lazy person who demands luxury and pleasure as a right. They were the Emperors of Rome who managed to kill themselves off through wine and debauchery and cruelty to other creatures including humans. Perhaps those Emperors of Rome have changed their disguise in the 21st century.

Maybe the slave masters who work in the drugs trades and prostitution have taken on a different view of the exploitation of others, but they also succumb to their dark thoughts, sooner or later.

The searches for the Holy Grail, the Ark of the Covenant and other relics have never been successful, as far as we know. What is spooky is that magical power has been assigned to them by people who should follow the tenet of not praising false idols. It becomes the construction of a grand myth. Why aren't the other knives and forks, plates and other cups given the mystical aura of the vessel Jesus supposedly drank from?

Your ally will not appear from a magic lamp but it will show itself as your best mate when treated with respect and with responsibility. It is within your mind rather than being trapped in a lamp or chalice. It is something that will advise you and care for you in return for you listening and sharing its benevolence with yourself. In real terms, it is your innate ability to make the right decisions for yourself.

It is your mother in its care and kindness and it is your father, sometimes seeming stern but really concerned with your wellbeing.

Derive Pleasure by Giving Pleasure

There are some people who derive pleasure at the expense of creating suffering for others. We all want to be happy but when our happiness comes at the expense of others then the balance is upset.

Let us take sex. When one partner is intent on getting pleasure for him/herself and ignores the needs of the other party then there is no long-term pleasure because the act does not fulfil the desire of strengthening the relationship. Prostitutes can get away with pleasuring a person without any self-pleasure. Porn actors are the same. It is all for the money rather than being an act of love.

An easier example is that of offering a seat on a bus to an old person or a pregnant lady. They get pleasure from being made to feel special and the seat donator should feel pleasure at being a good person who expects no reward.

The mental frame that is established says the good people are able to see the world in a better way for themselves and feel more positive and optimistic.

It makes little difference other than getting pleasure from mutual pleasures which lead to even more pleasure.

Principles of Balance

There is a balance in the Universe or in Nature or whatever you wish to call the unseen influences that exist. After Wars more male children are born than girls. Somehow nature redresses the

15

balance so that genders are close to being half and half.

If this balancing factor is so great, then it seems necessary to achieve balance in your life to succeed, whatever that means to you.

If you want wealth then you should share some of the extra money with those who need it more than you.

The balance is between the modern human who sits in the same body as the primeval ancestor. The modern human wants material things, (cars, big houses, money, etc.) whereas the primeval person wanted the satisfaction of fulfilling the emotional needs of hunger, safety and breeding to be at the fore.

This becomes the key to how we change our self-belief. This is the difference between wanting and needing. Needing is based on emotional values, wanting is material.

The Nature of Ambition
The nature of the ambitions you have is important. The attainment of your desires must be feasible. Feel your emotional desire for what you want rather than the means to get what you want. This needs explanation.

So, wishing to win the lottery to buy a car will probably never be fulfilled. Your thoughts alone are unable to influence distant outside events. However, wishing for a new car will give your mind a path to follow. This might mean working harder. It might mean stopping smoking to save money that can be used to buy the car.

Wishing for love is too vague. Working to achieve a meaningful relationship is a better idea. You have love already from your mother and father, your friends. If you want romantic love then define what that means to you.

Wishing for wealth is perhaps asking for too much. When we have money in abundance it can be like riding a War horse that is hell bent on jumping into flames. Misery is avoided by earning amounts that make us feel comfortable rather than filthy rich. Accepting that helps us to have achievable goals.

Belief
Success is when the imagined is made real by the belief that the outcome will be achieved because we have the confidence in our abilities to bring it about.

BEWARE...because failure fits this process as well. Therefore, never dream of the possibility of failure or it will most likely happen. Only plan for success, NEVER determine to fail. Create an attitude to win.

Make goals achievable so that they are believable. Confidence is a winning emotion for the imagined goal achievement. To be a winner is to be somebody who counts. The people who count are those who care. If your wish is for harm then just wait for the day when that harm comes back to you in whichever form it takes. Forget karma, that happens because you start to believe that there are harmful influences around and your mind searches for them.

Make your goals good for everybody and you will win in the longer term.

Live in the Present

You cannot worry about the past. The past is a teacher that will point out the errors that you have made and praise you for the things that you did well. These experiences can only give you the direction to take.

Learn from mistakes, learn from successes. The future proceeds from the present. It shows you that it is only how you are 'today' that will influence the future.

Persuasion is One Key

Persuasion is a powerful tool but you need to be clear about who you are persuading and why. At one extreme a gun in the hand would persuade a shop keeper to hand over the contents of the till, but this would also persuade the authorities to put you in custody for a long sentence when caught. A drug dealer might persuade you to 'sample' his wares at a low price or for free, and when he hooks you then the price of the sustainment of this addiction will be high, very high.

So, you need to bear in mind the need to persuade yourself that some forms of coercion are dangerous for the persuader as well as the persuaded.

What you must strive for is gentle and, ultimately, benevolent persuasion.

Gentle persuasion techniques

Enabling others as well as ourselves to be appreciated we have to become communicators of the goodness we hold. A good sales person has a huge battery of methods to gently persuade a potential customer to buy. One of the important methods is to approach the other person with a win/win proposition. This means that both parties benefit from the transaction. If the sales person goes for a 'I win/you lose' deal then ultimately the customer will be less than happy and will never operate with that sales person again. The other option is lose/win where the customer has beaten the sales person into submission and loss.

Gentle persuasion is where both parties feel that they have benefitted from the agreement.

Use the proposition that you are going to benefit the other party. Apply this to any situation that you might have to face. If you are going for a job interview then the potential employer needs to be persuaded that you will benefit them as well as yourself. An employer needs to buy your services that, in turn, will provide them with a net profit. If you want to invite a girl or man on a date then you need to persuade the other person that you will be good for their needs as well.

Selling is persuading somebody to buy what the seller is offering, hopefully to the mutual benefit of both parties. This is the base of communication between people. Perhaps goods, maybe ideas, sometimes liaison. We should look at some of the fundamentals in selling to achieve our goals.

Needs
In selling there are fundamental rules for success. The first is to identify the needs of the customer. These might include safety and security. Or status. Or something else. If you are selling a car to somebody then consider their different needs. A mother who drops her children off at school might need other mothers to be impressed with her family's apparent wealth. A young man

might need speed whereas an older person might need safety. If you sell speed to the older man then you are missing his prime buying motivation. A young man may need to impress his friends with the power of the car and, sadly, ignore safety. Motivation is the desire and the force to succeed. For motivation we need a goal, a need.

As another example, a man on holiday might identify the needs of a girl, also on holiday, as wanting to meet a man who will love her, marry her and give her a secure life. If he boasts about his sexual conquests then he will only see her back as she runs away. If he is kind, polite and caring then he might succeed in her accepting his dinner date. If the girl just wants a good time so she can boast to her friends about how many men she had on holiday then it is unlikely that she will respond to a man who talks about his joy in having preserved his virginity.

Features
Selling features is pointless unless the features are qualified into benefits. More of that in a moment or two. A feature is what most people who fail attempt to use as persuasion. It is almost always useless. So, the car salesman who tells the prospective customer that this particular car has four wheels, an engine and is red not only means that he thinks that the customer is colour-blind it also states the obvious to the point that the customer loses faith in him.

Benefits
What is in it for me? The potential buyer needs to know how they will benefit from the transaction, personally or commercially. Take note of the features and qualify them by using the statement 'which means…' in your thinking.

To the young man who wants a powerful car then the sales man says, "This car is bright red *(which means)* your mates will see you roaring down the road and will be jealous."

To the older man who wants safety he would say, "The bright red colour *(which means it)* will allow other cars and pedestrians to see you coming and they will be better able to avoid you."

To the mother he would say, "The red colour will be seen by the other mums and *(which means)* they will notice what a grand car you have."

And so on.

For the guy on holiday who wants to meet a solid girlfriend he would say how his lack of experience with women is because he has respect *which means* that he is a safer long-term bet than the party ravers around. If the same guy wants a quick thrill as a one-night stand then he can talk about his vast experience with lots of girls *which means* that the girl will think that she will have a night to remember. You may ask if what he is saying in either case is true. Then ask yourself how often you have exaggerated the truth.

Does this sound Machiavellian? Sorry, but it is this attention to detail that makes the difference between getting what you want or not.

Colouring In

When you have finished reading this book just think about how your life has improved. See yourself with the partner of your fantasies; You are happy with him/her. You cuddle when you want and you are cuddled and loved. You have found bliss and you have achieved your dream.

You might have the job of a lifetime. You see yourself in a position of authority in your office, perhaps in a car, perhaps on a commuter train from your nice apartment or house. Good, isn't it?

The moral is in selling the benefits. There is an old expression that states "sell the sizzle, not the steak." This is about using the most powerful asset that the human brain has, namely, imagination. Oddly enough, you very often get what you consciously dream you can.

Back to the car sales. It is easy to work out to whom the following pitches would apply:

"Imagine yourself on a warm Summer day with a pretty girl in the passenger seat, driving to the coast for a romantic visit to a sandy beach..."

Imagine that you are driving through the town and a child runs out in front of you. Luckily the brakes are so efficient that you come to a stop before you hit him. I dread to think what could have happened!"

"Imagine how your daughter's friends' mothers will admire you when you drop her off at school in this beautiful car. I am sure they would wish that they had come here themselves. Cars like this sell very quickly."

And in the other example:

"Imagine how it will be when the food is served tonight. The moon will be smiling in the sky and it will make the wine seem to sparkle..."

May I suggest you figure out the other scenario for yourself!

Closing the Sale

Being able to get a result is known as 'closing'. Agreement is needed for the deal to be finished. There are many ways to close and some are listed below:

The 'tea or coffee' close. A choice is given whereby the option of a 'yes' or 'no' answer is avoided.

"Would you like a tea or a coffee?" needs to be answered as a 'yes' or 'no'. The question, "Tea or coffee?" makes the assumption that a drink will be wanted and the only answer is which one will be accepted.

"Will a credit card be OK, or would you rather use cash for the car?"

"Would you prefer dinner at 7.30 or 8 o'clock, tonight?"

Also will-power is self-persuasion

Control yourself. Appear confident.

Suggestion, Another Key

Suggestions must always be positive, never phrased as a negative.
"Do not think of blue elephants", is one example. Are you

thinking of blue elephants? Instead you say, "I am thinking about my new house."

Suggestions should be in the present tense; it is deemed to be happening **now.** If a suggestion such as, "I will stop smoking" is made your mind says, "OK. So, we carry on smoking until then." In the present tense you say, "I am a non-smoker, NOW." There is then no need to carry on smoking.

Appearance

'Clothes maketh man' is an old expression about appearance. Rather imply that your wardrobe should be replaced, it is important that a smart person is never seen as a dirty tramp if you want to feel and show self-esteem. 'Naked people have little or no influence on society.' Mark Twain. Dress for the occasion, your clothes define the person you are and the person you aspire to be. Be smart when you go out. Impressions are made in your own mind as well as others.

Politicians always seem to wear suits. This shows they are "educated, polished, sincere and caring" Cynicism states that the truth is not always on show.

Actors on chat shows sometimes wear jeans and could appear to be over casual but the jeans are always smart, well pressed and make the statement that the actor has **control** over their lives. It is a non-conformist conformity that makes a statement.

This principle applies to all five senses. Consider:
How you look.
How you taste.
How you smell.

How you sound.

How you make physical contact.

These lead to the sixth sense which is intuition or gut feel...How do you feel? If you feel less than successful, make the changes you need...NOW.

Control

The foundation of misery is being controlled by outside forces. Some we can fight things such as bad habits; others we have little influence over, such as taxes.

You might feel:

Controlled by yourself, smoking, drinking, drugs, fetish etc.

Controlled by others.

Controlled by circumstances.

Controlled by fear. Irrational fear is better thought of as an inappropriate negative emotional response.

Controlled by corporations, including the church.

Controlled by the suggestions of others with advertising.

The answer is to take control and live your life as the pilot rather than as the passenger.

You tell yourself that you are the master of your destiny, that you make the right decisions to move your life forward and that you are doing that NOW.

Curiosity Killed the Cat

Did it? Curiosity is the force that brought man down from the trees as it is for our relatives in the ape world.

If we had assumed that the 'right way to do things' was to be maintained as the status quo then we would never have used fire as a tool rather than think of it as a threat. The bronze and iron ages would never have happened. We were curious and so we still are. This enables us to look for different answers to problems.

If you feel stuck in a rut then give your curiosity full rein to find a way out that suits you. Be curious, be creative and be successful.

If curiosity killed the cat then the answer it found brought it back to life. Perhaps that is why cats have nine lives !

Knowledge is Powerful

Knowledge is never reserved for the 'wise'. Remember that they are wise in certain subjects and are naive in others.

Gain knowledge about what your goals are. Be an expert in your field whether that is academic or practical. Yet never become a bore by expounding your theories to others. Let your knowledge be a powerful tool in building your self-esteem.

Have the Attitude to Win

Boxers know how to win by knowing what to do. Not renowned for their academic prowess, boxers have the confidence to perform their skills within time and energy limits. That is their knowledge, which is their strength. As a quick note, in reality boxers are, in the main, bright people. Remember the wit, humour and skill of Muhammad Ali.

At another end of the scale, Stephen Hawking never gave up thinking, he was a curious (possessed curiosity rather than being odd) and a brilliant man despite his handicaps.

What these two icons had in common is that knowledge, in whichever way it is held, is truly powerful.

Possessing Things or Possessing Life
A warrior can only use one weapon at a time. If he has three bows then he can only fire one of them.

"Having or being?" is a great question. When a person places their priority on just owning and having things, then there is no joy unless he/she does something to utilise them. So, as an example, if a pop star buys a house in the West Indies, the South of France and an island in the Pacific and sits in his apartment in New York doing nothing but drinking himself into oblivion, is he happier than a middle aged couple using their old camper van every weekend to see their friends, countryside and cities?

We are searching for quality in life (emotional) rather than quantity (material).

Repetition of a positive wish gets through to your mind. Repeat and repeat your positive thoughts.

One way to do this is with affirmations. State what you want and then speak that desire to yourself as an aim already achieved. Remember that time is a function of logic and obeys laws of past, present and future. Emotion is free of time restraints so the emotional future is the emotional present.

Avoid negatives in your affirmations as mentioned earlier. (Language for positive thinking is a huge topic and will be covered in detail later on.)

Affirmations reset your emotional framework. So, a single person who affirms that they are capable of being in a good relationship will be more ready to establish one than a person who feels they are single because they are not good enough for one.

Celebrate Your Achievements

Be proud of achieving something. Forget the idea that 'pride comes before a fall'. These are controlling words of those who are jealous of success. If you ever watch interviews after events like Wimbledon, it is a factor with winners that they talk about how well they have done. This is not to boast but more about building their self-confidence for the next game.

Health

Tell yourself how to be healthy. Do the obvious things with stopping smoking, taking exercise and eating properly. But tell yourself that you have good health. You have heard of doctors telling patients that they have 3 months to live and the patient will set the calendar to the date on which they will die. Their minds, sadly, follow the plan. Others will ignore the date and out of bloody-mindedness will live for years and years.

Be bloody-minded enough to be healthy. Let the negative suggestion be what dies rather than you.

Wealth

Having wealth is more than having lots of money. It can mean having love and satisfaction in your life.

What is the difference between being wealthy and being comfortable?

There is emotional wealth and material wealth. The drunk beggar feels wealthy and happy if he gets enough money to buy his next bottle and the playboy feels wealthy and happy when a woman becomes his patron. Neither of these are recommended as a way to find happiness.

Your wealth should be based on having enough for your own happiness, which is emotional gain rather than material excess.

Happiness

If you had a very serious illness and you were given a cure you would be ecstatic about it. This would also apply to a person or people you know. Happiness can be defined as the lack of misery, sadness or upset. This gives a sense of achievement which makes us proud. Avoid feeling smug. Share happiness with others as a gift.

Voice of Authority

Sometimes we "need a voice of authority." We will do as we are told if we respect the person who gave us the instruction. Examples include sports coaches who will push athletes beyond the point where they would give up. Doctors are heard when they tell people to stop smoking or to lose weight, albeit including an "or else" caveat. You will know the "or else" involved in stopping smoking or in losing excess weight.

Add your own voice of authority in your endeavours, including the 'or else' part in your instruction. After all, you know best.

You Are Good Enough to Do This

Stop telling yourself what you cannot do, just say what you can do. Never expect to be perfect the first time. Skills need to be practised to become skills. We learn from our own errors in doing what we want to achieve.

Two Worlds
There are two worlds. There are the emotional and the material planes.

The material world is about work and work is about profit. Profit is about the individual. So, a coal miner sweats to sell his labour for money. The mine owner sells the coal for profit. The coal merchant sells the coal for profit. The coal miner buys the coal and burns it.

The banks "look after" money. They never buy it from the ordinary person. The money that is not owned by the banks is loaned to people and companies for profit (interest). They might give some of that interest to the owner of the money.

The emotional world is where nice things should happen. Feeling good about helping somebody without expecting material gain is positive. Being able to sleep without a bad conscience is wonderful. The emotional world is about being rewarded in your life as it is. Putting things on hold for rewards in the next life is never a positive thing to do. That is part of being controlled. Enjoy your life. Be happy now.

Be Your Own Boss
Being your own boss is the dream. Being in control of your own life rather than having somebody tell you what to do. But being your own boss must therefore involve you telling yourself what to do and ensuring that it is done. The real benefit is that you choose the tasks and the outcome.

The Three Daily Checks
The following helps you to plan and review your activities in a constructive way.

Take a piece of paper
At the top, write:
What will I do today will move my dreams forward?

Then hallway down, write:
What am I doing today to move my dreams forward?

Near the bottom, write:
What have I done today to move my dreams forward?

Every day start with the top question and jot down what you will do. Monitor your progress through the day and when you finish review what you have achieved. What is left over goes forward to the next day. Rather than being a list of chores, your prompt must be a catalyst for creative thought.

Things To Do
Define goals to achieve...chunk down.

Make decisions with positive outcomes

Make up your mind.

Be resolute.
Determine to set boundaries.
Reveal problems and resolve them.

Options/choices. Avoid prevarication and set realistic courses of action. For example:

'I want to go on a date with a specific movie star or pop singer'. Very unlikely to happen. No, instead 'I want to go on a date with a pretty woman or handsome man'. Achievable.

The punch line is that rather than desiring an ethereal force to bring about change it is the responsibility of the individual to do that. That eliminates blaming something else. Also, magic is about creating illusions of truth. Your magic is in the use of techniques to do that.

3

BELIEVING IN YOU

AUTHOR NOTE. THIS PART IS INCREDIBLY IMPORTANT. BECAUSE WE TAKE OUR LANGUAGE PATTERNS FOR GRANTED, YOU MUST RESIST THE TEMPTATION TO SKIP THROUGH THIS, PLEASE. TAKE IT SLOWLY. THE BENEFITS ARE ENORMOUS.

CHANGING YOUR LANGUAGE
(AND YOUR THINKING)

WHEN WE THINK, it is like having a conversation within our own minds. This is our internal dialogue. Those thoughts are 'flavoured' by our emotions. We run a process of risk evaluation at the same time. When we are walking, we recognise ruts in the road, or dark corners where dangers might lurk. However, when we worry, we think about problems that might become reality without having rational justification.

We know that our thoughts can change our feelings. Fear is an emotion. Those fears that seem to come from nowhere have their origins in our unconscious thoughts rather than from a recognised stimulus. We react as if the threat were a real thing. Rather than thoughts they become 'feelings.' Yet when those thoughts are of pleasure, we relax.

The language that we use for our internal and external dialogue is important for our well-being and for dealing with the problems that underlie our anxieties and lack of self-belief.

Within modern culture there are four things relating to language which work against us, but which we can use to our advantage when we know the secrets.

1. We live in a society that sells problems for a living.

Can you imagine taking your car to a showroom where you are told that the vehicle you have is perfect? No! They might suggest that the mileage is high, or the engine size is unsuitable, or that the fuel consumption is uneconomical. They will identify and explain the 'problems' that you have and then they will solve them by selling you a new car. This applies to most trades.

Even salaries are paid because if your position were vacant, the company would have a problem in getting its necessary work done. We survive by solving problems, and then by maintaining the possibility of the problem recurring.

2. We use words too cheaply.

We sustain our personal problems by the poor use of language. That is, we use words too cheaply. We pepper our speech with brief idioms that communicate on a superficial level, but have different deep-seated meanings. My favourite example of poor language that is counter-productive came from a client who said: "Perhaps I really ought to try to think more positively!" That sentence contained all the reasons why she would find it difficult to do so.

The words 'perhaps', 'I really', 'ought' and 'try' are weak rather than positive. They are 'failure' words. They appear to state a positive objective but they infer that the goal will be missed. If the intention is firm then the sentence becomes, "I think positively."

3. We like negatives!

We tend to use strange constructions that are based on double negation. Why do we say, "that's not a bad idea" rather than "that's a good idea", for example?

Negatives are necessary for rational disciplines. Mathematics has to have the concept of negatives to work, but we are dealing with our emotions. As you will see later, negatives are unable to dismiss problems but they potentially intensify them.

4. We make our lives conditional.

We make statements to ourselves and then accept them as solid truths. Superstitions are a good example. "If I walk under a ladder then I will be unlucky" or "a black cat crossing my path is a good omen" or a bad one in some cultures! We make our lives conditional. If X happens then Y will follow.

This happens with anxiety states. "If I go to the supermarket then I will have a panic attack." I have even heard the statement, "I know that I will get a panic attack two and a half hours after taking my beta-blocker." Surprise, surprise! She did until we changed her language. Suggestions are quickly made and adhered to. When we make the wrong choices with suggestions then we pay the price.

Breaking Out Of Thinking Traps

Our self-talk is full of traps. Most people have heard of the word **'affirmation'**, a positive phrase or suggestion aimed at changing the ways in which we think about ourselves. The most famous one is "Everyday, in every way, I am getting better and better." However, very few people actually use positive affirmations. Most of us are very adept at using negative ones by accident!

35

We develop and hold onto erroneous beliefs that distort and change our behaviours and attitudes.

Sadly, we are wonderful in reinforcing negatives by our thinking. When we make negative suggestions to ourselves then we run a huge risk of believing them. Things like the following need to be ruthlessly destroyed. "I am unlucky", "I am ugly", "I am a loser", "I will get fired because I am useless at my job."

There is a way to break the negativity of our self-talk. We use very positive techniques for changing our language, which in turn modify our thinking, emotions and reactions. These are based on eliminating negative words and conditions. We replace them with a language and thinking that contains beneficial intention and positive intent.

The rules and steps are simple and easy to remember.

Look at the sentence **'I will NOT panic** (or not get angry/become anxious/get stressed, etc.) **in the supermarket'** (or in the car, at the restaurant, at work, on a date, etc.) This seems as if it will work.

However, within that short sentence there are three fundamental errors of thought that will bring about the opposite response. From working through this example, we see how to turn our goals into language that communicates the correct message to our minds.

1. 'I WILL' puts the hoped-for solution into the future. The future is tomorrow, next week, next year, whatever. This tells us that whereas relief will be found, it is unlikely that it will help us

<u>now</u>. Putting that hope into the future reinforces the problem that you currently have. It becomes a self-fulfilling prophesy.

The first rule and step is to place your problem into the past tense.

If it WAS a problem, then it follows that it has gone. Your mind gives you the unconscious positive suggestion, or affirmation, that you need. You put the solution into the present tense by using the words 'I' and 'NOW'.

The affirmation then becomes: 'I **used** to panic in the supermarket (or whatever) **BUT NOW, I feel peaceful, safe and relaxed.**'

If you find that your mind tells you that your problem still exists, then argue with it! Repeat your affirmation over and over.

2. The second rule is to lose the small word **'NOT'** in suggestions. (It works in prose but is a no-no in self-talk. Although we know what positive suggestions are, we fail to use them. Instead, anxiety sufferers use negative suggestions accidentally. These maintain the problem rather than giving a solution. When we are thinking about behaviours, our minds seem to be unable to recognise negatives. When we use the word 'NOT' we often create the opposite outcome to that which is desired. Let me give an example: **'Do NOT think of blue elephants!'**

It is likely that you thought of blue elephants. It therefore follows that the sentence 'I will NOT panic in the supermarket' is understood as 'I WILL panic in the supermarket' because the instruction is contained after the word 'NOT' in the words 'panic in the supermarket'. The word 'not' has no effect in changing that instruction. The blue elephant example told you, after the word 'NOT', to **think of blue elephants.**

Use a sentence that affirms what you want to happen rather than using a negative in an attempt to negate the unwanted effect. To repeat, lose the word 'NOT' from your thoughts. To replace it state the result that you want in positive terms.

A quick note. Whereas the word 'not' is to be avoided in suggestions and self-talk dialogue, it is permitted in negating things as in 'blue is not green'. And, people who tell me I am stupid, ugly, etc are not nice.

3. The third rule, and next step, is to omit any reference to the problem when you are used to putting it into the past and when you have stopped using the word 'not'. The last part of the sentence is a reminder of the problem and it is emphasised. '...panic in the supermarket.' It tells you to do what you want to avoid. Never feed a problem by talking or thinking about it. Starve it to death. Make it an exile, something that used to cause upsets but which has now been eliminated. Eliminate the problem and tell yourself what you want to happen. 'In the supermarket (or in the car, at the restaurant, at work, on a date, etc.), I am calm, confident and in control.

PUTTING IT ALL TOGETHER:

1. Make your suggestions positive, current and relevant to the solution. Ignore the problem completely. It is something that you used to have, but now you are fine.

2. Avoid certain other words such as 'perhaps', 'ought', 'should', 'maybe', 'if', 'might', 'probably' and 'try'. These imply either failure or weakness.

3. Make your internal dialogue strong and assertive. Tell yourself what you want to be by telling yourself that what you once wanted in the future is how you actually are, **now**.

4. To summarise, model your suggestion on the following, "In the supermarket I am calm, peaceful and relaxed." Stop your language from telling you otherwise.

Can you now see why 'DON'T PANIC' is the WORST thing to say in a crisis? 'STAY CALM AND RELAXED' is so much better.

Write down your first thoughts about how you would like to feel. Now review what you have written and edit it to eliminate the words that affirm your problem. Rewrite your aims in positive words that contain the solution in the present tense. Check your words with the lists given a little later in this chapter.

Become your own editor.
Editors check the constructions of words and grammar before publication. When you think, check how you are thinking. Your objective is to ensure that your thinking and spoken words are positive and direct. Delete any negatives that you find in your inner and outer dialogues.

Two negatives do not make a positive! Yes! I have used the 'not' word. As written above, using the word 'not' in a sentence with positive intent reverses the meaning. However, attempts to change a negative sentence into a positive one are ineffective.

To demonstrate this, it is better to give an example. If we use the sentence "I will not stay calm" rather than "I will not panic" then they will both have the same effect of signalling alarm. That little word is a negative influence whichever way you look at it! Throw it away. Refuse to use it. This becomes easier with time, I promise.

Read, watch and listen to advertisements.
Good advertising copywriters are skilled people who have to communicate messages which will evoke positive action. They sell the benefits of a product or service. You will notice the absence of weak words such as 'try', 'don't', 'won't'. However, notice the abundance of affirmative words such as 'will', 'can' and 'now'. Make sure that you analyse high quality advertisements. The most adept advertising professionals will have written these. Make a list of the active and optimistic words and add them to your vocabulary. Compare them to advertisements in local newspapers from small businesses. There you will spot the less effective use of language. Remember that advertisers are setting up needs to be resolved by you purchasing the product or service that settles the need you were unaware of before.

Some of you will be thinking that the word 'try' is used in advertising. 'Try our product and if you do not like it, get your money back.' This works on the idea that when you try something then the bother to get the money back will put people off making the effort. Here the word try invites people to test. It implies that the manufacturer has confidence. It probably has an effect. The manufacturers think the risk is worth taking because we enjoy receiving but dislike the effort of returning something.

However, 'try to lose weight with our product' is different. Here the failure sense would be implied as happens in most cases of the use of the word. In short, lose the 'try' word!

Listen to politicians.
Politicians sell voters the apparent problems caused by their oppositions and then they offer the solutions that they think that they have. Watch news programmes to explore the language used. Notice the cryptic meanings of phrases such as 'their employment policy is not working', the hidden emphasis being on 'is not working' suggesting that there will be unemployment. The follow up would be 'our employment policy will bring rich rewards to our voters'. Remember that our culture sells solutions to problems that we create. Politicians are coached in the use of language by experts behind the scenes. Their speeches are scripted rather than heart-felt in lots of cases.

Listen to positive people.
Listen to the words and expressions of people who are confident. Their self-esteem is reflected in the language that they use with others. It follows that their internal dialogue is as assured as their outward speech. Copy them!

WORDS, WORDS AND WORDS TO AVOID

Try. Implies failure. Remember that when somebody says that they will try to see you at 3 o'clock, that gives you at least ten more minutes before they will actually arrive.

Not. Creates a negative suggestion as already mentioned.

But. When used in the present tense to explain why something will fail. In this way, 'but' creates the negative reinforcement of the problem. For example, "I would like to drive on motorways, but I panic."

Perhaps. Conditional expectation of failure as in "perhaps I will get better".

Might. Conditional expectation of failure as above.

Maybe. Conditional expectation of failure as above.

Should. Conditional expectation of failure as above.

WORDS TO USE CAUTIOUSLY

All words which put action or intent into the future. They maintain the problem in the present time. However, if they reflect an intent that was previously missing and a time frame, they are useful. For example, "I will go to the doctor tomorrow" or "I can relax when I visit the hairdresser in an hour's time."

Can. A positive word that refers to the future but is sometimes conditional.

Will. A positive word that refers to the future.

If. This makes the intent conditional. An example of bad usage is, "if I meet somebody new, then I will be anxious." An example of better usage is, "if I use positive language then I will be in control." However, it is best to say, "I use positive language and I am in control, now." (See below.)

WORDS TO USE

(I) **Do.** A positive word in the present time.

(I) **Am**. A positive word in the present time.

Now. A positive word in the present time.

But (when following placing the problem into the past tense.) Used this way, 'but' creates a positive affirmation. For example, "I used to worry about driving on motorways, but now I feel calm, confident and in control."

Avoid. This is a word of positive intent. "I used to get angry with myself, but now I avoid criticising myself by recognising my true value."

As. A conditional word that implies a result. For example, as you read this book you find it is helping you to improve your life.

FOLLOW THE RULES, PLEASE

Rather than just reading the language rules given above, become familiar with them, understand them and then adopt them.

They are:
1. Place your problem into the past tense and the positive outcome in the 'here-and-now'.

2. Lose the word 'not', and any other 'weak' words.

3. Then, omit any reference to the problem. Define the solution in 'strong' words.

As you change the language of your thoughts, then;
Your mind becomes more relaxed;
Then your body posture changes;
Then your breathing changes;
Then your life changes...for the better.

4
RELAXATION AND COPING

Like me, you will have received emails selling the greatest relaxation techniques ever, for scary price. Forget them, snake-oil salesmen. Relaxing is part of our nature. We do it when we are asleep and we do it naturally when our minds are at peace.

LEARNING TO RELAX is straightforward. Making the time to relax on a regular basis is the thing which causes the most problems for people. It is easy to write that you should meditate for ten minutes in the morning and for twenty minutes in the evening. People with that much time to spare should be stress-free in any event!

Therefore, the following is a realistic approach to relaxation for people who have little time to spare. This can be done within any time-frame and in any location which is safe.

When you are relaxed, repeat suggestions and affirmations over and over in your mind. Use your imagination. The relaxed feelings you have opened the door to your unconscious mind and you have now the language to communicate with it.

"EASY-MEDITATION."

Rather than to achieve a state of nirvana, our aim is to experience the calm, confident and in control state on a regular basis in order to reduce anxiety and self-deprecation. Hence the name.

Getting ready. Find the most suitable place that you can. It might be an armchair, settee, bed or the floor. Equally, due to circumstances, it might be a railway carriage, your office or your car-seat in a rest stop. There should be no rules for relaxation, or time limits. Tailor your resources to your circumstances.

HOWEVER, NEVER DO THIS WHEN DRIVING.

The basics.
Make yourself comfortable and safe. If you are using your car whilst parked up, for example, lock the doors. If you are in a train, ensure that any valuables that you have are secure.

Positioning.
Sit or lay in such a way that your body is as open as the surroundings and decency permit.

The tradition meditation position where you sit on the floor with your legs in the lotus-position is fine if you can put up with the discomfort! However, just sitting with the soles of your feet together and your knees as far apart as possible opens up the pelvic area and encourages deep abdominal breathing almost automatically. If you sit on the floor with your legs together and outstretched, you will notice how much this restricts your ability to breathe into your stomach.

When you lay or recline, make yourself as open as you are able.

Run a muscle-check. Relax your neck, shoulders and stomach. Ease out the thigh and calf muscles. Separate your ankles and open your legs as much as your situation allows. Let your arms droop down or rest them on your thighs. Open your hands.

46

USING YOUR SIX SENSES.

1. **Proprioception (or mental massage)**
This is the sense that we are least familiar with by name, but we know what it is when explained. It is the sense that, amongst other things, will know where the light switch is in the dark. It is an awareness of where parts of you are in space.

Start with the top of your head and work down to your feet. All animals prefer to be stroked downwards than upwards. Do it to your partner, dog or cat. You will notice a difference. Concentrate on breathing slowly into your abdomen. Ignore your upper chest. That will fill on its own.

Feel, with your mind, every part of your head every time you breathe in. As you breathe out say to yourself, **"I am calm, confident and in control, now."** Or whatever positive thing you want to say to yourself.

Feel, with your mind, each part of your head including your hair, ears and nose as well as the muscles. Move down your body doing the same thing, in whichever order you like, but include every part of you. You will finish with your toes. When you get there enjoy the feeling and, if you wish, include one or more of your other senses.

2. **Visualisation.**
Imagine whatever gives you pleasure; a beach, a waterfall, swimming with dolphins or a person. Anything! Imagine it as a picture or as a film. Involve yourself in the scene or watch it as an observer.

3. Hearing.

Listen to imagined birdsong or waves or add your favourite music as a soundtrack. If you are travelling, listen to the rhythm of the train wheels.

4. Smelling.

Smell anything that you can. Imagine freshly cut grass, perfumes or flowers. To some, the smell of a wet dog is relaxing. Alternatively, smell the real odours around you.

5. Tasting.

Add a favourite meal or the taste of a blade of grass in your mouth.

6. Feeling.

This is the sense of feeling the world outside of us. The textures, temperatures and shapes of things, real or imaginary.

This process of focusing thoughts onto pleasant things takes us away from the worries that haunt anxious people and puts us into a safe environment where the calm, confident and in control state takes over. You relax for as long you have time to do so. For some it will be twenty minutes, for others two. There are no rules. The only thing that is important is that you do it.

RELAXING WITH REAL EXPERIENCES

Our memories work with associations. The above exercise brings about relaxation by using the imagination with associations. We can reverse the process by using real objects to stimulate pleasant memories of relaxing events. The following are examples of things that may be used to help relaxation.

1. Proprioception.

This can be anything from dancing to Tai Chi. Movement is relaxing. Feel, with your mind, where your limbs are located in space when you move.

2. Visualising.

Look at landscapes, pictures or photographs that have pleasant connotations. Draw, even if you feel that you lack the talent.

3. Hearing.

Listen to recordings that inspire images. Listen to music, birdsong or wind-chimes. Hear children laughing. Listen to what appears to be silence and find sounds within it.

4. Smelling.

Gently sniff foods, spices, flowers. Grade them. Find categories and rank them in order of preference.

5. Tasting.

Roll foodstuffs and drinks around in your mouth like a gourmet or wine taster. Define the differences between sweet and sour. Determine the ingredients used in the things that you eat.

6. Feeling.

Touch and feel the different textures of cloth or modelling clay. Feel the different wall coverings in your house. Caress plants and/or pets.

ROLE MODELLING

Become a method actor. Pretend that you are acting out the role of a confident person, free of stress and problems. You find role models everywhere. There are people that you admire. Copy their posture, their ways of walking, talking and breathing. You find them in real life, television and films. Watch politicians making speeches.

Admire actors in demanding parts. These successful types are acting out their lives. They were born in the same way as you and me, but they have dressed themselves in the behavioural costumes of what they want to portray.

Do the same. What happens is that the fantasy gives an escape from the negative way in which you regarded yourself. It shows you that when you act a character, you become that style of person. You give yourself positive experiences, which you can grow from. You change your approach from running and hiding to that of control.

The main essence of relaxation is that of occupying the conscious mind to the extent where it stops from being judgemental about the suggestions you want to pass to your unconscious.

Prepare suggestions carefully and make them when you feel relaxed and receptive. It is as if you make yourself an observer sitting in a room while you talk to a confidante, free from interruption or interference.

5
FINDING CONTENTMENT

THE PARALLEL UNIVERSE IN YOUR MIND

A parallel universe is just in the imagination, isn't it? It is a place where things are as you wish them to be.

If there is such a place, we should ask the question "Why are those lucky so-and-sos having all the fun?"

Too mystical, yet your mind seems to make your world turn out to be the way you create it. The rich always have money because that is the way they see their lives being. Happy people seem to find happiness in their lives because they want it.

So, does a parallel universe really exist? Who knows? There are theories in physics involving protons, neutrons and string theory that are only in the minds of physicists. But there is a mental parallel universe that we can all find.

If we want to access this place where everything is better than the one we live in we have to create it in our minds, in our thoughts and then it starts to exist in our reality and begins to affect our day to day lives.

Our thoughts can create the reality in which we live. Negative thoughts will bring negative results. But why?

Remember the old expression, 'be careful what you wish for'.

What you tend to look for is what you will find. A man who looks for apples in an orchard will find them hanging from the trees because he looks upwards and forward. Another who worries about snakes in the grass will miss the apples because he is looking down fearing a bite, but in reality, he will not see any snakes but might imagine he hears a hiss or sees something moving in the grass. The first man walks away happy, the second worried.

The orchard remains the same but the expectations of the two men are so different.

FUNDAMENTAL DIFFERENCES

With people there are two fundamental elements in behaviour.

The first of these is the fundamental nature, the fixed behaviour of somebody that is difficult or impossible to change. The metaphor of a leopard not changing its spots is important because this describes the basic nature of a person who, despite promising change, is actually trying to put on a disguise to gain advantage knowing that the change is short-term. The patterns in the fur and skin of a leopard are cosmetic so any change is only superficial. Even if the patterns are changed by scarring from a fight with a lion or hyena the nature will remain the same. It is the inner core of the big cat that has to transform.

The second fundamental element is essential change. This is where something has happened that has shown the person that the old behaviour is damaging and destructive. This is where the person needs courage to see that the enemy is within, not outside. There is no fight to win but there is peace to be gained.

The person has to recognise the negative behaviours that have caused conflict and then discharge them into the past where they can dilute and disappear. Look to the future to see and feel the peace, love and harmony that is to be gained. Then incorporate that into the present and a fundamental change will have taken place.

Once again, we can look to nature for an example.

A dragonfly starts life as a nymph, a sweet name for an ugly and greedy predator of other insects, some crustaceans and even small fish as it hunts in its watery habitat. Then one day, perhaps after regretting being such a fierce and ugly thing, it climbs from the water and finds a place where its skin splits and a dragonfly emerges. This is the difference with fundamental change. The water inhabiting vicious nymph changes into something beautiful that flies. The dragonfly can never become a nymph again. Something ugly turns into something beautiful. What happens is permanent change.

This is metamorphosis. The same thing can happen in the mind, with the emotions. Here it is called catharsis. It takes something powerful enough to bring it about, but it is possible and it is wonderful.

To make those changes, it is necessary to remove the old ugly thoughts and behaviours from yourself (the nymph). Then the attractive and transformed 'you' emerges.

How to do that follows on.

6

REMOVING YOUR BAGGAGE

THE FIRST STEPS

It is said that there are only two causes of misery; having things that you do not want and not having things that you do want.

If you want a happy life, and most of us do, the following will show you how to stop making it unhappy. It will help you to find real contentment in your life.

First of all, we need to identify what your baggage is and where it came from. Have a look at your garbage bins. Some are for waste that needs to be disposed of permanently, things like food that has become mouldy or rotten. Then there are things that can be recycled such as glass, metal cans, some plastics. They have been used and are now unusable as they are, but can be crushed or melted and turned into something of use and value. Some things can be repaired and made good.

Your emotional baggage is like that. Some things are rotten and are unrepairable. They will probably relate to your experiences in the past. Get rid of them. Some things can be mended or recycled, however.

This book is about dealing with your problems, your need for self-belief, self-esteem and confidence. If your partner has problems, then you can talk about how you recycled yours rather than lecture them. Preaching will dig up issues they have and you will be the target of blame for raising an issue. Imagine looking through your neighbour's bins and telling them what they should do to improve what they are doing. Maybe, just maybe, you could tell them what you have done to recycle your own garbage as a story without implying that they should do the same. We humans hate being told what to do. We have to make our decision to change.

It is necessary to look through your emotional baggage piece by piece. Yet there is one fundamental thing we need to address as a priority.

EXTERMINATE YOUR INNER CHILD

This piece will sound hard, even upsetting but please read on.

We have all heard about rescuing the inner child. Why should we? It does not exist as a person; it is an emotional handicap, an encumbrance that drags us down.

It is not a child, it is an ogre that sits in our minds and gets its revenge on us as the closest adult. When we refer to it as a child we are tempted to feel sorry for it and if it needs rescuing then we mess up our lives in terms of guilt. No, the inner child has to be renamed as the little s*** that lives in our heads and has tantrums and makes us have tantrums as well, while it laughs at our misery.

The child that you were may have been affected by careless parenting, abuse, jealousy, sibling rivalry, bad schooling or whatever, BUT that was you as a child. Children are mostly sweet and lovely, but there are some elements that can be obnoxious. Now you are an adult and the little so and so wants retribution on those who represent the perceived nasty people earlier in its life.

It was not you but, hey, there is nobody else other than you and the people you love that it can gets its kicks from by screwing you up. As the so-called inner child is not a child or even a human being, dismiss it, banish it and be rid of it.

You cannot change the past, it is true, but you can prevent yourself from being reminded of the past. If you shout or swear at somebody, especially those that you love, then you are taking out the payback of an imaginary kid on somebody. The more you hurt that person then the happier that 'kid' becomes. When that little monster goes back to sleep then you revert to the way you should be and you are left with nothing but regret.

Allow yourself to be the grown up that you are. Destructive childish behaviour will destroy your relationships, and eventually you. Those childlike horrible behaviours were used purposely when you were a kid and you learnt how to exploit them. They do nothing but hurt you now.

Be bold, get rid of the spoilt brat inside your mind. It exists no more than your childhood goldfish that died and was buried or flushed down the toilet.

Remember the good things about your childhood as if watching an old film BUT never keep the parts of it that are like a horror film that will give you nightmares.

So please keep reading to find out how to do this.

THE VENTRILOQUIST'S DUMMY

The ventriloquist's dummy is a great metaphor for the malevolent inner child. It sits next to a person and says outrageous things, swears and has an attitude of superiority to the person who is working it. People laugh at the embarrassment caused to the operator. Because it is removed as a source of pain to the audience, the onlookers love it all.

If you want examples, watch or read the plots of great films such as Magic with Anthony Hopkins where the dummy, Fats, takes over the consciousness of the ventriloquist and ruins his existence.

Let us call this thing Dummy, because you cannot see it but it is part of you but it seems impossible to get hold of and remove. It is a part of you that encourages you to be nasty and spiteful. More of Dummy later.

The story of dummies creating hurt is reproduced in many films. The malevolent dummy is a physical representation of the so-called nasty and malicious inner child that is produced by feelings of hurt caused in childhood. It wanted unconditional love and a million other things.

Tantrums and threats work for children. A tantrum gets loads of negative attention. Attention is what they want whether negative or positive. Of course, when the tantrum stops they get positive attention as the parental relief kicks in. It is like stopping banging your head against a wall. It feels better when you give it a break.

Threats are things like telling a parent how much they hate them and they will threaten to do something bad unless they get what they want. What they want is attention.

Compare the above to a cat that sits on your lap and for no reason scratches you and runs away. When it wants food again it will sit on your lap and purr for attention and because it is being sweet and nice, it will get what it wants. Is this how you are when you are angry? It is probably the same as when you were a child.

The great image to create to get rid of those childhood experiences that still control your life is that of separation of two elements; you as you **are**, and you as you **were**. That child represents the way that you were and still wants to control your adult life by behaving as the horrendous brat.

In your mind either throw the ventriloquist's dummy into the crusher or take it to bits and recycle the parts into something useful and helpful to your life.

The other way to look at your dummy is as the 'monkey on your back'. Getting it off is an expression that says get rid of your problems by taking control of your life without interference from a monkey interfering with what you want.

If you are worried that there are too many mixed metaphors, Monkeys, Inner Child and the Ventriloquist Dummy, these are used to expand the point that the something that haunts us needs to be eliminated.

This thing, Dummy, represents past hurt and it becomes a

vehicle for blame. It is tempting to refuse responsibility for your actions because you feel that it is all somebody else's fault. Blaming the past still removes the blame from you in the present time. No, it is you who is making the mistakes, not the imaginary enemy from the past.

That is history. You are the only person who decides how to act in the present part of your life. You cannot change the past but it can show you what to avoid. Remove your history as a model for how to behave. You are no longer that brat who lived in your memory.

In the next section titled, KILLING THE DUMMY, we shall run through an exercise to remove the nasty inner child from the mind for ever and to prevent this thing from spoiling lives in the future, once and for all.

KILLING THE DUMMY

OK, this sounds bizarre but please trust me. It works.

We referred to the removal of the malevolent inner child, aka Dummy the personal ventriloquist's dummy who made us into the angry and spiteful person who has suffered hurt and heartbreak as a result. Remember that the nice childhood influences of love, support and warmth will remain.

As an aid, think of your life as a nice garden pond full of pretty fish that represent your good memories. Then, out of the blue a piranha appears and starts to devour them one by one and every time you introduce a new happy memory from the present time, that gets eaten too. Simple solution, remove the piranha and allow the life in your pond to flourish.

We will visualise an outcome.

Read through the following and then copy the process in whichever way you can in your mind. You should be in a comfortable position, breathing gently and with closed eyes. There are no rules, just be at peace.

*****

Imagine that you can see all of the negative factors in your life, those things you have done and said to hurt others and yourself. Then see them as pieces of smashed debris on a smooth and level floor. If you cannot visualise something that is able to be thrown onto the floor then imagine that you are writing that event, hurt or person onto a piece of paper that you can screw up and discard onto the floor.

Dummy is near you. Break the dummy into bits and throw them onto the floor as well. You might imagine pained, childish noises of protest. You might hear pleading; you might feel sorry for this representation of the inner child that was once you. Be strong, ignore everything. It is not a child; it is an evil life spoiling representation of the causes of your misery made from clay, wood, plastic and cloth with a few mechanical parts. Ideal for recycling.

Now sweep it all up. Vacuum it up if you want using an industrial scale machine. Hear the cries of pain and hurt you caused. See the tears you made flow, your own and others. Enjoy the silence from Dummy as the brat is now unable to speak or make a noise.

Put all of this debris into a big hessian sack. Use a dustpan and brush to get every part packed away.

Tie the neck of the sack with string and drag it to a big bonfire. Put your sack on the tinder, kindling and wood. Imagine it is a replacement for the Guy Fawkes dummy

(If you are not familiar with the bonfire night on the 5th November in Britain, it is when an effigy of a traitor has been burnt for hundreds of years.)

Take a match and light the fire. Stand back and watch.

Remember this is not a person you are burning but the harmful emotions that have stained your life. It is a decontamination of your mind.

Colour the images in with every sense you have. Smell the smoke, hear the crackling as those bad things get consumed by the flames, taste the cleanliness in your mouth after those sour words have been erased. Touch your head, now empty of those nasty thoughts and watch as the flames die out just leaving a pile of ash.

Breathe gently and be proud of who you have become. A person in control of what you say, do and think.

Meanwhile, we will continue with recycling the emotional damage into something extremely valuable.

7
DEALING WITH SPECIFIC PROBLEMS

Anger

Aggression is dangerous. We have to look at anger from two sides. If you are an angry person, then you need to find out what causes it to happen. Is it from jealousy, not getting your own way, drink or something else. Sit and remember when you have been angry and what caused it. Think about it when you are not angry. Write the causes down because they are the things you need to work on. Avoid blaming others, it was you who became angry.

In a similar light, if you live with a person who suffers from anger then seek help. Anger can grow from bad words to physical injury. Ensure that you are in a safe relationship, please.

Arguments

It is easier to start a war than to end one. Likewise, it is easier to destroy relationships than it is to build. In an argument words are said that wound. An argument is a fight with words that can escalate into physical action. Neither party in an argument will win. Like a boxing match, both people will walk away with mental and emotional bruises.

The best thing is to move away and think about the potential consequences. If you walk away and are followed, explain that you need space to calm down.

Criticism

Do you criticise yourself and/or others too much? Do you feel disappointment rather than a failed attempt to do something right?

Are you the recipient of criticism?

In either case you must discuss the issue with the critic or ask yourself why you see catastrophe in the efforts of others.

Remember that criticism damages the ability to feel contented. I have a saying that is, 'the most perfect thing about humans is our lack of perfection.' This drives us on to make progress. If the great inventors of the things in life that help us such as penicillin, the light bulb, X-Ray and so on fell victim to criticism, then where would we be? You are less than perfect so striving to be so is a waste of time. Acknowledge that you will make mistakes and use those to learn from.

Drink, Drugs

Alcohol, cocaine, heroin etc. seem to be ways to escape from an undesirable reality into a, perceived, better way of life. It is, in fact, a destructive method to deal with issues and a sober head will always resolve problems more effectively.

If you have a problem with drink and/or drugs then sort out the issues that you are escaping from and ditto if your partner has a similar problem.

As with anger, drugs and alcohol destroy lives and relationships. Jail can beckon for theft or violence when the usual social norms are exceeded. With younger people fired with alcohol and testosterone, the bestial drive to dominate and fight becomes paramount. This is seen with drugs such as cocaine as well as alcohol. Cocaine use leads to paranoia and this in turn, can lead to aggression.

Jealousy

Jealousy is said to be the third leading cause of non-accidental homicide across different cultures.

Unlike envy, a jealous person is worried that something they love, whether physical, personal or monetary, will be taken away by somebody who is perceived to be better. A jealous person might be envious of another but the jealousy is directed at what is considered to be the possession of the jealous person.

Sometimes a partner is causing it because of their infidelity or it is self-invented because of lack of self-esteem.

There is more about jealousy later.

Loneliness

'Negative emotions like loneliness, envy, and guilt have an important role to play in having a happy life; they're big, flashing signs that something needs to change.' Gretchen Rubin

When you feel lonely you can either wallow in self-pity or do something about it. Doing something, or anything, will pay huge dividends.

Orders

Request rather than order actions and behaviours from others. They will feel less threatened and will be much more likely to do as you ask with enthusiasm rather than resentment.

If you are being ordered around, then accept that you are a person rather than a spare part. Explain that soldiers obey orders for the safety and protection of themselves and others. Orders in your normal life are inappropriate and should be modified to requests that can be worked on.

Orders are telling you to do something with an assumed authority than is impolite. If you order somebody to stand up they will look puzzled and surprised but if you request that they stand up with an explanation, then they will be more than willing to do so. Take this example with you as a response to anybody ordering you around.

Resentment

Resentment is when you carry your feelings of disappointment and fear with you as a grudge and you replay those feelings over and over by building the negative feelings.

Those feelings hurt you and not the other person. Work through why you are feeling resentment and dilute the feelings associated with it. It will never help you to carry the pain you are experiencing and you should do your best to make the state of mind one which is favourable to you.

Sarcasm

If a broad insult is a big cutlass, then sarcasm is a sharp thin and pointed weapon used to prod and hurt. If you harm another person with any sort of verbal sword, then you will push that person away from you. You will gain nothing from your seeming subtle use of words to make your point.

Discuss issues that you might have in order to find an outcome that suits all parties. Sarcasm never shows how clever you are with your wit and wisdom; it hurts YOU instead.

Sexual demand on you.
There is a scale along which this topic runs from somebody asking to make love, to a person asking you to do something that revolts you. The first end of this scale can be discussed and agreement one way or the other reached. 'Perhaps tomorrow if you are feeling tired, maybe Saturday night and so on.'

In the second case, depending upon the manner in which you are told to do something you do not want to do you can reply with, 'If you don't love me enough not to do that, then where does our relationship go?'

If the other person is too persistent then they have a major problem because they are only thinking of their own wants without consideration for you. Think long and hard about that relationship.

Tantrums
We have talked about the child that haunts us. A tantrum is the weapon of a child to get attention, usually negative. Children do that, adults do not. It is about anger at not getting your own way and it involves screaming, shouting and being obnoxious in either spoken or written words. A tantrum is one of the things that will destroy relationships faster than most other bad behaviours.

Time
Boredom. Do something. See the list of possibilities you have in

the section titled **THINGS TO DO.**

We can feel that we have too much time or too little. Swap and balance the two. Use the excess time to do the things you think you have too little time to do and vice versa.

Work
Organise your workload into things that have to be done straight away and prioritise the rest. Some tasks can be easily put out of the way by doing them or by putting them lower down your list of things to do.

Worry
Analyse and discover in detail what you are worried about and then resolve those issues. These can include health. See a doctor rather than worry. Once your issues have been recognised and treated then you can stop worrying.

Maybe it is money in which case set budgets that account for income and expenditure. Trim your expenditure to your minimum needs. Easy to say, I hear you comment but the only other option is to live with the status quo and carry on worrying.

Happiness
A lack of a feeling of happiness is perhaps the reason you are reading this book. Go back over the points and action them. Reading is pointless unless you commit to making positive changes.

The first thing to get rid of the biggest negative influence in your life, and that will be identified in the next section.

JEALOUSY

To repeat, unlike envy, a jealous person is worried that something they love, whether physical, personal or monetary, will be taken away by somebody who is perceived to be better. A jealous person might be envious of another but the jealousy is directed at what is considered to be the possession of the jealous person.

Jealousy often signifies a lack of trust. Trust is the foundation stone of love. This is trusting that the partner will be faithful and includes a sense of security about the future. It also signifies a lack of confidence.

In primeval terms, jealousy would have protected the nurture of children. A man who left his mate for another woman would have left hungry children behind so the mother would have been wary of competition.

A woman who left her partner for another man would have left her mate and would have taken his children with her so the man would have been worried by attention to his mate by another man.

Jealous people might want to fight physically or verbally. This is seen with young people who are taking early steps in mating routines when they are dating. They assume that competition has to physically fought off. It is also seen in the control of a partner by force as if training a wild dog to walk to heel.

A question to ask yourself if you suffer from jealousy is have you been unfaithful yourself? Sometimes a jealous person will project their own behaviour onto a partner. If he/she has been unfaithful then it stands to reason, in their thinking, that their partner will do the same thing. Quite often the jealous person is the one that needs help to settle the relationship down.

Ex-partners can be jealous of new partners. This is when the 'ex' is considered to be a possession and that somebody else has stolen them. This applies to an inanimate object but never to a person. If a man or woman leaves then it was for a reason.

There are people who have a predisposition to jealousy from experiences in childhood, sibling rivalry and so on. Perhaps they had bad teachers who showed favouritism. You may be a person who has been cheated on before and who has developed mistrust as a protection mechanism.

You need, always, to look for root causes of this problem. You need to unravel the tangled knot in all cases before progress can be made.

You must build trust and confidence. This goes with self-esteem. If people think they are inferior to a partner, colleague or a friend then they have to see why that thinking is false and destructive. Again, relativity counts. A person will have attributes that makes them equal at worst to a perceived rival. The need is to build self-belief.

PAST PRESENT AND FUTURE

It makes a great deal of sense that we should look at the past and sieve out the bad bits. However, those pieces should be discarded leaving the better memories to work as a foundation for the present and future. The past is important but if we keep looking at it as if looking perpetually in the rear-view mirror when driving, we will crash. An occasional glimpse behind, suffices. The important thing to do is to look at the future as if it is a clear and clean road.

Problems have to be dealt with in order to move forward but there is a point when the problem has to be considered to be something that we HAD. This means that the desired outcome exists in the present.

Affirmations work because they recognise a future desire in the present tense! This strange paradox works. When we reflect back then we carry our problems with us as if they are a huge part of our very being. One powerful way to bring about change is to develop positive affirmations. These have to be set in the present tense because a change that will happen in the future means that the status quo still presides over the current situation.

We want a release from our problems and an affirmation will work after we have dealt with the causes of the problem. The way in which we think and act can be changed by encouraging ourselves to define new goals rather than living out old frames of being as our model.

"I will become positive" is weak against, "I am positive" because it still affirms the negativity with which we think about ourselves.

If we tell ourselves that 'I will get better' and use that as a suggestion or affirmation, we are implying that we still have the problem. If we believe that the problem is something that we had, but <u>now</u> we are free of whatever that problem was, then we <u>have</u> a positive affirmation of a new state.

To use verbal pictures, we have to uncouple the railway carriage that carried our problems and let it slide into a siding so that the rest of the train can move forward unencumbered. To explain more with a different picture, if we have an old car that is troublesome, it is never enough to assure ourselves that one day we <u>will</u> get a new one. We need to acknowledge that we <u>had</u> an old car, but <u>now</u>, we <u>have</u> a new one.

The past is where the problems started. The past is what often influences the present. We can recognise problems that were caused in the past but we are totally unable to make any changes to our history. Yet, we can learn from it and move on. When the present time is seen as being attached to the past then the problem remains.

However, when the future is fixed to the present time and a gap is made with the former issues then we can separate them from the past. This enables us to move forward unencumbered by our history but mindful of what could happen if we repeat previous behaviours.

RELATIONSHIP SPLITS

I will discuss this from the point of view of my work as a therapist.

'I will change. I will never do it again. I do love you' and so on.

These are some of the words that were spoken by people to their partners before they came to see me. They were looking for magic! The client hoped that by seeing a therapist the problem would be resolved with a third party.

Sometimes those words were meant as an intention, other times they were said as a stalling mechanism for a failing relationship. I will differentiate between the two extremes.

With the first type, problems within a person can be dealt with and resolved but I was never able to fix the consequences. If an angry client lashed out with words, then the promise to change might be honest and I could potentially help. The thing I was unable to do was to offer to persuade the wronged partner that the angry person had changed for good. I could never be part of the promise that the problem had been resolved to ensure the safety of the hurt party. I would never confuse the two issues. My job was to treat the anger rather than act as a relationship guidance counsellor. That would be an extra brief, to be treated in a different way.

The second type would be asking for a respite rather than help. Hoping that time, and my apparent help, would restore the status quo and I was under no illusion that I would be helping nothing but a stall. The reactions of the client would have told me which scenario I had. A highly co-operative and open client who showed genuine remorse would have featured with the first type.

An arrogance and lack of co-operation signalled the second. I was always very wary of the second type. I was very conscious of the dangers that I could have caused. I questioned that type of client deeply to find out what their real motives were for seeking help.

Then, if necessary, I explained fully that I could only help people who were genuine in their search for treatment and then I did my absolute utmost to turn the client towards the direction of a happy future with the problem resolved in depth.

Everybody should seek happiness but in order to do so they have to admit that they are the cause of upset and that only by **their** change would they find it rather than set up a smokescreen that would hide their behaviour for a while until the dust settles. Then the original problem would, once again, raise its ugly head.

Reject before being rejected.

There is another phenomenon that I encountered. I refer to this as 'reject before you are rejected'. This is a self-esteem issue whereby the client will be lonely because he/she is without friends. They will have been hurt in the past and they adopt the strategy of never committing fully to a new relationship in case they are hurt again. Thus, they will push a new friend or suitor away when the relationship develops to the point where the client feels vulnerable.

The rescue came from building the client's self-esteem to where they could become able to take the risk of rejection happening. It becomes a 'win, maybe lose, but be happy' situation rather than a 'lose/lose result come what may'. Find the cause of the feelings of rejection and build confidence. If a parent or a boy/girlfriend was the cause, then other people that you have yet to meet will be different. Their acceptance of the rejected person, perhaps you, will have a totally different foundation.

Ownership

Sometimes after a relationship has ended one of the two people will claim ownership of the other party. If one person leaves a house, they might want to keep a key to enter the house whenever they want. The excuse might be access to children or to a toolkit. This, of course makes new relationships difficult, if not impossible. That is why the partner who has left will do it. They are jealous and possessive. They want their cake and they want to eat it as well.

The person has to gain enough confidence to change the locks, take a Court injunction or other action to stop it. I never told a client to do this, my job was to help the client to be strong enough to do it of their own accord. My advice was never given.

Needless to say, the partner in a relationship that has been ended by another person will have feelings of depression. This is because they have lost somebody that they wanted. There is a loss of hope in restoring the relationship and of ever having another that is successful. They will blame themselves and search for reasons. This process will drag up every dark thought in their psyches.

The hope that you must believe is that things will get better. Life goes on. What must be accepted is that the person has to be able to prepare for, and accept change.

EMOTIONAL PANIC ATTACKS

A panic attacks happens as the result of the fight or flight response. They happen when adrenaline rushes into the bloodstream and prepares the body and mind for action. I find it necessary to add two other components, those of defend or freeze. These happen when we perceive a threat and we will react in different ways which are driven by hormones rather than logic.

I shall explain more.

If an animal attacks you then you will fight it off or run away. Sometimes you would freeze like a rabbit caught in headlights, or you would defend yourself.

We are talking about emotional attacks rather than physical ones.

Fighting is lashing out with words, insults, accusations and a whole array of behaviour that is aimed at hurting the adversary, as perceived. Sometimes this can be a physical attack which is a loathsome as it sounds. Add alcohol into the equation and it gets as bad as it can. Often the threats are imagined rather than real. I used the words perceived threat rather than a real one, above. We can go back to jealousy and other misinterpretations of the reality in which we live.

The imagination is strong. We see it with the fear of flying, where people imagine the worst outcome from the safest form of transport. It is also the main component of horror films where we see the monsters and never think of the actors dressed in rubber masks on a film set.

Flight is when we want to escape, get away and look for protection or to hide. Running often provokes the attacker into becoming angrier. There is another way to escape and that is to dive into a bottle of alcohol or to hide by using mind altering drugs. Often these things make people aggressive so the parties involved are both on a war footing, often over nothing. The flight response turns to fight.

Defending is attempting to ward of an attack, verbal or otherwise. In doing so the attacker can, again, be aggravated because defending is easily turned to an attack. Defending denies the attacker what they want and they are likely to become more verbally or physically aggressive. In that case, you need to escape.

Freezing is where a person does nothing from their great sense of fear. This can encourage the attacker to come back with the same behaviour time and time again because they appear to have got off scot-free. To an extent they have and they will carry on repeating their behaviour on subsequent occasions. This is often the hallmark of domestic abuse where it seems easier to put up with the violent actions and words than to escape to safety.

How to deal with them
If you are the aggressor then you have to deal with the fear and anger that builds into the sense of loss of control and makes you panic, recognising one or more of the indicators mentioned above.

If you are the victim of a person who reacts badly in some situations, then you need to encourage that person to seek help to overcome the anxiety that makes them panic and become aggressive. If that does not work, then you should seek urgent help if you are at risk.

There are coping methods that are described in THE ART OF CALM later in the book. These really help.

8
FINDING CONTENTMENT

This part of the book shows you how to find real happiness and contentment without buying into false hopes that create anxiety because rules are given and the inability to follow them and get results will cause stress and fear of failure.

If the so-called law of attraction worked by drawing on the resources of the Universe by asking and then believing and waiting for the result to happen then we would be living in a world that is free from war and suffering. The majority of humans want peace, they dream of it and what has happened? Nothing. If we want something, then we have to invest in effort to achieve our goals. In order to attract something then we need to know what we want and be willing to work to achieve it. The assistance that the idea of a law of attraction gives is that it encourages people to focus on what they want to happen. Then the mind has a clearer path to follow. Rather than criticising it, I recommend the idea of focus as runs through this whole publication but, my reservation is only in that the users are expected to believe in outside forces that in all probability never exist. The benefit is from within the mind.

Sure. We all want health, wealth, happiness, peace, a nice house, joy, love, a good partner and recognition. And so we become easy customers of a myth. We are sold the Law of Attraction as if it is real magic from the Universe, a supernatural force. It becomes the secret that we need to buy into. Like a magic trick, it is mostly illusion.

We have a different choice to make. You can lay in bed and dream up what you would like OR you can get up and do something. This book will give you guidance for achieving what you need rather than creating a fairy tale of wishful thinking. What you need to do is to focus your thought on your goals and you can do that without a whole spectre of rules and methodology that are usually sold.

With a simple focussing on your desires you open your mind to recognising what is out there already but which is ignored because we have so much information coming in that the mind becomes over protective,

Perhaps you need more money, a better relationship or you just want to be happy and glad to be alive.

If these, and other things are what you need then keep reading...the answers are here. This is a down to earth guide for finding contentment written by a therapist who has improved the lives of many people.

'Contentment is not the fulfilment of what you want, but the realization of how much you already have.' Anon.

Now there are lots of suggestions for the reader to look at and think about. They are like items on a menu. You can pick and choose rather than consume them all. You can always come back for more. They will apply to you when they are relevant to your needs.

The purpose of the words that follow is to share the means to find contentment for you. As you will see later, sharing is an important component in your recipe for creating a better life.

You will not be told what to do. Orders do not lead to contentment. In fact, giving and receiving them causes problems, as previously mentioned.

This part of the book is short and to the point, deliberately. The author could waffle on to fill pages but the need to find contentment is in the 'here and now' rather than in a lengthy study course that will take unnecessary time to finish.

Please read through the points that follow at your own pace and do your best to make any changes that you feel will help you.

Contentment is available wherever you live, however much money you have, or do not have, and with whomsoever you share your life with or would like to.

This is not a part of the book full of instructions that must be obeyed. Instead it is a straightforward guide that is full of helpful tips for achieving contentment.

The changes you will make may seem unusual at first but really they are straightforward. The end result is always worth the effort. If you do not perfectly match the recipe, then you will still end up with something worthy and satisfying.

The ingredients that you will need are listed as we move on. They come as different flavours and quantities. But unlike a food recipe too much or too little will never spoil the outcome but making the effort to use the components will achieve a better outcome for your life.

WHAT IS CONTENTMENT?

The answer is never a simple one. It does not come as a yes or no, or right and wrong. It is an amalgam of lots of different elements, like in a recipe for fine food.

When I have asked people to define contentment, they have always described it in emotional terms rather than financial ones.

Being contented is having peace of mind, feeling good about your life and your surroundings.

It is also about how you are at this moment in time and will be in the future.

SAVOUR THE MOMENT

You are living now and you will live in the future. The past has gone; it cannot be changed. There are no options for 'replay'.

If you are searching for contentment then it will arrive when you want it to or, even better, now.

If it will happen tomorrow, next week, next month or next year it follows that you are unhappy now. Let us think of today as the beginning of the change that is taking place.

That means that you can view today differently. There is an old saying that states that 'a long journey starts with a small step'. Why assume your change is a long journey? It can be instantaneous. You are dealing with your emotional well-being rather than with a physical distance.

Concentrate on the things you can change rather than those you cannot. Newspaper headlines are based on bad and sad news, the items that sell newspapers rather those that inform the reader of what is good in the world. Their purpose is to make profit from advertising and the more lurid and eye catching the headlines are then the more copies they sell.

If the summer is hot, then you are told we are experiencing a heatwave and people will die. If it is cold, then we will die from illnesses brought about by germs attacking us. If it is raining, then we will worry about flooding.

Enjoy these changes in the weather and take precautions if it is going to be severe and dangerous. It does not affect many people but it worries us enough to watch the news and buy newspapers.

'Headlines, in a way, are what mislead you because bad news is a headline, and gradual improvement is not.' **Bill Gates**

Learn to savour the moment. If your past is sad then see a great future growing from today. The past is finished. The future starts with every moment that happens from now. It is, and will be, different when you make it so.

If you are only aware of the 'bad headlines' in your life then, together we will turn the page to find the good news.

Dismiss those things that have made you unhappy, they are yesterday's news. Begin your better life...now.

WHO CONTROLS YOUR CONTENTMENT?

There is a very definite relationship between control and contentment. This is not one sided. We can feel controlled by other people, rules and by money. Then there are those people who seem to have control but may fear that they will lose it.

Part of control is restraint. The prevention of something or somebody's behaviour is at the heart of the matter. If you control somebody, then you will upset them and likewise if you are controlled then you cannot do what you would like to do.

Break the chains that bind you and keep you from enjoying your life.

What we need is **balance** so we are not over controlled and so we do not control things or events to excess.

Sometimes you will be the person who wants to control and the reaction you get is opposite to the one intended. If you tell jokes all the time, then rather than getting laughs you will alienate your fellows. Sharing jokes is fine when you are telling them in the right context and as long as you listen to the others you will be welcomed.

The same applies to conversations. Listening and sharing is the most important thing to do.

Part of contentment is having others around you who are also contented in your company. If you hog conversations or lecture rather than share your chat, then you will push people away. There is a wonderful saying that expresses it beautifully; 'You have two ears and one mouth, use them in those proportions.'

If you make that a rule, then the end result is usually 50/50 but you will be seen as a person who others can have a talk with.

Remember the Simon and Garfunkel song, "The Sound of Silence":

People talking without speaking,
People hearing without listening.

Some people will only talk about themselves and anything you say will be returned to you in terms of their experiences without wanting to hear what you have to say. They need to learn how to listen. If you are like that, then you need to listen and to show genuine interest in what others are saying.

Feel like a member of a modern species. In our primeval history life was about hunting, cooking, sex for breeding and sleep. Now we have complex language that can express emotions.

For contrast, we can take an example from nature where an animal like a stag has to live with discontent. The dominant animal has to fight to retain his females that he services for his short term pleasure and then he has to protect his place against his competition. His longer term contentment is always controlled by others.

Key Points
Seek balance in your life. Avoid being negatively controlled and avoid controlling others.

Control the amount of control that exists in your life either incoming or outgoing.

Listen more than you talk. People will like you more.

SHARING AND HELPING

We live in a complex social world where we like to know where we fit in.

Sharing is not about giving something away so that you lose. It is about gaining. It is a mutual exchange of anything from money, food, emotion and friendship.

Imagine opening a bottle of wine. If you drink it all then you might lose control and lose friends. If you share it then you will spread pleasure in a generous act. Sharing has huge benefits. Rather than wine, imagine you are sharing joy, happiness and contentment.

Another example is a pizza cut into slices. Would you eat the whole thing in front of hungry friends? No, you would offer slices to them and they would be distributed evenly. All of you would be happy.

Money
Bill Gates has made an absolute fortune and he has shared much of it with others by way of foundations and charity gifts. Is he content? You bet.

There are huge companies that have a profit-sharing system with employees. This leads to a higher level of job performance and satisfaction.

What is not being suggested is that you share your money unless you can afford to but there are some universal hints that giving and sharing will result in gaining a return. Perhaps that is emotional rather than financial but it offers contentment. Certainly happiness is enhanced by being as generous as possible when needed.

Feeding your pets and wild birds will never end in them saying 'thank you'. You share your money and time in buying food and putting it out and they will give you a sense of satisfaction because they have enriched your life with beauty and song.

Love and Sex
Love making is a mutual pleasure because the sharing of bodies is satisfaction for both parties. Sex, however can be one sided. If one partner demands sex for their own relief, then the other person is left feeling used. That emotion of being exploited will return to the user in different ways.

If love making cannot be a shared joy, then it is necessary to find out why one of you is eating the whole pizza and drinking the whole bottle of wine.

Talk to each other but most importantly listen.

Time
Away from love making and sex, share time to share experiences. Find out what your partner and other people like doing. Even if what they want to do is contrary to what you like to do, the result you will get will far outweigh any discomfort

you felt from giving happiness to somebody. If they like walking on a beach, join in, for example.

Things
Share vegetables with friends and neighbours from your garden if you have an excess. What you will receive will be a kind thought if nothing else.

Share your lunchtime sandwich with the birds in the park.

Stop worrying about the trivial things in life and allow yourself to enjoy the bigger joys of life.

Lonely people do not have others to share with but people who share are less likely to be lonely.

Key Points
Sharing is a great way to gain happiness and friends. Two or more people in a joint enterprise makes it so much easier.

Love making is sharing whereas sex for one person's relief is hurtful to a relationship.

SCALES OF CONTENTMENT

There is a timescale for contentment.

Short term pleasure will leave you wanting more and more because you are feeling good in the present time and you want it to continue.

Long term contentment is when it is spread over your life.

Perhaps it is not as intense as the short boost but it will be a goal to aim for as it lasts and lasts.

There are components of contentment which vary.

Perhaps laying in the garden in the sunshine. Maybe going for a walk, eating, meeting others. These cannot all be done at the same time but they will set the balance of contentment at an optimum level for you.

In short, be contented doing whatever you are doing without worrying that you are not doing something else. Live in the happy moments. The practise of Mindfulness follows this path. We should live in the moment, but I think we should also dream of the happy future. Why not?

You always have choice. I have seen a 94-year-old woman making sure she walked a small distance to keep her body moving. I also know a 92-year-old woman who only moves around when she is on holiday. And finally, another younger person who is happy to sit and watch the television and be waited on by her partner. These are three different facets of contentment. There are no rights and wrongs, no judgement. However, there is a balance in the larger picture.

If you want to read a book or listen to music and it makes you happy, do it.

Allow things to happen in your life that satisfy you. Do what you feel like doing if it does no harm to others. There are no extra rules other than being honest with other people and to yourself.

It is your life after all, it does not belong to others.

Key Points
Look for contentment now and in the future. It is your life so do what makes you and others happy as long as it is legal and it never causes discontent in others.

SETTING YOUR MINDSET

Your mind is like a loyal dog. It will do what you train it to do. If you train it to scare people, then that is what it will do.

If you believe a house is haunted, then sooner or later you will see a ghost.

There was a Tommy Cooper joke that says he went to the doctor and said 'it hurts when I do that'. The doctor then says, 'well don't do that'. When you tell yourself that you are unhappy or miserable then you will feel that way. Stop doing it!

Believe in the idea that contentment is achievable and you will find contentment. Belief in a good future brings it about.

There are some thinking traps that need to be disabled. The next section shows you how to do that.

Key Points
If you have trained your mind to believe you are miserable then you can train your mind to be positive and happy.

Believe in your present and future wellbeing.

EMOTIONAL CONTENTMENT

Emotional contentment is reliant on your emotional state rather than the amount of money you spend.

It is about being happy with the way things are in your life or are becoming.

There are wealthy people who are content and there are wealthy people who are not. Similarly, there are poor people who are happy and those who are not.

Remember what was said before. 'There are two causes of misery, having things that you do not want and not having things that you do want'.

The discontented wealthy people want to make more money and/or have more control over other people. Perhaps they worry about the financial crisis in the World or about signs of aging and buy the sometimes catastrophic results of cosmetic surgery.

Maybe they want to live in different parts of the world but their friends and family are more geographically fixed and so become remote. And so on. Have you ever wondered why so many pop stars and actors take to drugs and alcohol? A mansion in California can become a lonely place where the stars are surrounded by false friends.

The happy ones live within the natural processes of life and travel through time with dignity and acceptance of their chosen fate. They can be reassured by their personal resources and feel secure enough not to require pleasures that have to be bought.

The same applies to the happy less well-off who enrich their lives with friends and family. Rather than going to concerts or the theatre they can be happy with watching events on their television sets and sharing a meal and a joke with similar folk.

Not too long ago, in England there was a 'celebrity' who was held in high esteem and was worth £11 million ($19 million). He was convicted of child abuse. In my head and in the heads of most people this made him totally worthless as a human. That is the true value of the man. I laugh as I wonder how he will spend all that money before he dies, probably in prison.

Compare him to a man I saw in Mumbai on a business trip that I was making. I had to take a bus between the International Terminal to the Domestic one. From this bus I saw the slum shacks at close quarters, some housing people and one housing about eight buffalo. These sheds, by Western standards, were horrible. The inhabitants, however, looked relaxed, almost like tourists on holiday in the Mediterranean resorts, keeping out of the sun. They were happy with this way of life. I suppose they were in a community where all were equal, no snobbery, just sharing life. A man stepped out of his shack and started to pee onto the dried earth. He had no signs of having money but he had a look of peace and contentment on his face, one that said he felt sorry for those of us on the bus hustling and bustling to make our pay cheques. An artist would have painted that look as a thing of beauty. He would have accepted a few rupees as a gift but he seemed happy without it. Money was not his goal. He just enjoyed his simple life with his family and friends.

Sadly, we value things by their cost and we value people by their assets. These are transient, hollow measures of worth. You have what you have, be grateful. When you are greedy you will be in that place where you want more for the sake of possessing it. That brings discontent.

Few are the rich people who do not want more money. They cannot reach the ceiling and they are unhappy with their wealth. Far better are the rich people who share their wealth for the benefit of others.

Getting back to the 'celebrity' child abuser for a moment, he was probably content that his perverted needs were satisfied without any consideration for the feelings of those he abused. His short-term selfish contentment has turned out to be the cause of his misery, now he is in jail. Sadly, the hurt that his victims felt and feel will not go away with his conviction but they might feel some contentment that they helped to bring about justice and that they have, at last, been believed.

His reputation and respect were demolished in the moment of being found guilty. It is a shame that it did not apply to the other celebrities and politicians who used their money, power and influence to wreck lives before they died, but hopefully it will restrain others.

Key Points
Contentment is an emotional thing that never depends on the amount of money that you have. It is free.

Selfish contentment will blow up in your face. Share the joys of life with others.

NOBODY IS AN ISLAND

Some lives can be like living on a desert island even when we are surrounded by fields, buildings or people. We can feel isolated wherever we are.

Even Robinson Crusoe was grateful for the company and help shared by Man Friday. At first, they could not communicate because they spoke different languages. This problem took time to overcome, but in the end, they shared a good and strong relationship.

In your mind you could imagine living on a desert island and wondering who you would like to be there with you. Your island could appear as your relationships with the other people on near but separate islands. What could you do to build a bridge between the them all?

On your island what would you need and what would you like to abandon? You would not need money because there would be nowhere to spend it.

Answering these questions can set you in a different frame of mind about what you would like to do with your life.

Contentment is not just a singular personal thing. It is built in a nest of contentment from others so you are sharing your peace of mind.

It is also feeling part of something but compare belonging to a gang that sells drugs to young teenagers with working for a charity that rescues drug users. Who would feel more contented when they are in bed and there is a knock on the door? This is related to feeling fulfilled in what you are doing.

Be contented doing what you are doing. Sitting in the garden shelling peas is boring to some but a joy for others.

Dream what you would like to be doing that would make you happy and then work towards that objective and it will happen. Moaning about what you do not have is destructive; planning a happy future is the start of a contented time.

Key Points
Think about what you would need to feel really contented and then make that dream a reality by taking positive actions.

SOMETHING TO LOOK FORWARD TO

If you want contentment look forward to it with your inner eyes, your imagination. Whatever we desire is available if we consider our needs without greed or harm to others.

This is not some sort of spiritual or new-age spell, it just seems to work because you set your mind to recognise people, things and events that will help you to achieve your goals.

We receive so much information that the mind has to ignore in order to sort the wheat from the chaff.

When we dream of our aims then it as if a door in that wall of rejection is left open for ideas and hints to gain access. The expression 'closed mind' fits this explanation well when it is joined to 'open minded'.

An open mind is receptive to new ideas and clues.

The first step is to loosely define what you would like to have in emotional terms. The concrete resources you need will follow on behind.

It goes a bit like this:

If you want a holiday in Florida, imagine yourself and others on a beach in the sunshine enjoying the smells of the ocean, the feel of the sand, the sounds of the waves lapping on the shore, the taste of the food you will find there. Hold these sensory images in your mind and you will find coincidences that will help you to achieve that dream.

Keep it in those exciting images of the result. If you imagine the physical money you would need to pay for it, however, then your dream will bring no result apart from frustration at not getting it.

Money is a tool for trading with no existence in the fabric of the mind in terms of what it can buy. You have to see and feel the result you are looking for rather than the simple tool for buying it.

Dreams are always emotional and are a powerful force.

There is a quote allegedly by Goethe that says:

"Until one is committed, there is hesitancy, the chance to draw back. Concerning all acts of initiative (and creation), there is one elementary truth, the ignorance of which kills countless ideas and splendid plans: that the moment one definitely commits oneself, then Providence moves too. All sorts of things occur to help one that would never otherwise have occurred. A whole stream of events issues from the decision, raising in one's favour all manner of unforeseen incidents and meetings and material assistance, which no man could have dreamed would have come his way. Whatever you can do, or dream you can do, begin it. Boldness has genius, power, and magic in it. Begin it now."

How this works is beyond logic but it seems to bring results. My belief is that we pick up clues from random events about our goals when we have that focus in our unconscious minds.

Key Points

Use your imagination to conjure up the emotional results you desire.

Allow the events and people that will help you to achieve your dreams to enter your life and thinking.

INNER PEACE COMES FROM OUTSIDE

Meditation is hard. Finding inner peace by using the traditional meditation methods takes a lot of effort. Rules have been established for body position and repetitive mantras. Like lots of esoteric knowledge, it is too full of impediments to be easy or fast.

We will take a shortcut.

Think of contemplation instead. This is about looking at things and thinking about them. Not in a candle staring way but admiring things around you. Examples could be watching birds feeding in your garden or in a park. It could be watching a fishing float bobbing around in rippling water. It could be watching people in a non-scary way in a shopping mall while you sip a cup of coffee.

In fact, think of contemplation as a form of daydreaming. Take inspiration from things around you and apply those thoughts to your situation that you want to improve.

Key Points
A great way to enjoy your thoughts is to take peace from your surroundings and mix them.

Contemplation is a fast way to find relaxation and inspiration.

THOSE WHO SURROUND YOU

Think of yourself as being in a small boat on the open seas.

With true contentment in yourself then the water around you is calm. If you are surrounded by discontented people, then the water becomes choppy and you are feeling less secure and comfortable. If you upset other people then a storm breaks, the water becomes rough and threatens to sink you.

Think of your friends both current and past. Friendships are worth their weight in something more precious than gold.

There are ways to keep in touch with people. Letters, emails, postcards, seasonal greetings and, of course, the telephone. Rather than waiting for them to contact you, take the initiative today. The spoken voice is heard more loudly than a social media message because the voice has the extra dimensions of tone, speed and volume.

If you worry that they will not want to hear from you then you have postponed something that might be as heart-warming for them as it is for you. We are social creatures by nature. They need contact as much as you and perhaps they are worried that you do not want to hear from them. Be the initiator.

Key Points
Surround yourself with friendly people.

Keep in touch with your friends and family.

THINGS TO DO

Allow happiness to happen. It is your life, not others.

Accept the benefits of doing something for others and yourself and you will receive the benefit yourself. In other words, if you want to go for a walk, sell the idea to others by talking about seeing the ducks, smelling wild flowers, getting some exercise rather than talking about walking which has less appeal.

Go to a concert or art gallery where you might meet somebody who shares your interests.

Going to bars needs to be done with caution as you might meet somebody whose hobby is drinking or they are there because they need somebody to be sad with, or to pick up somebody.

You could take an evening class in something that interests you. Others in the class will have similar interests to you by being there as well.

You can do things for charity. You will meet other people and you can feel useful to society. It also gives you something to occupy your spare time.

Key Points

If you normally do nothing and you are bored and lonely, do something where you can meet like-minded and happy souls.

Being happy is not a sin, it is your right.

CREATE SOMETHING

Creation of something is a powerful part of human existence. We gain a huge amount of pleasure from making something physical or mental. The following are suggestions for you to consider creating. Your mind might say that you lack the skills to do so but the attempt is important. We are not all poet laureates, bestselling authors, artists, master mechanics or engineers but we do not need to be.

Build shelves or flat-pack furniture.

Fix a bicycle.

Paint a room of your house.

Write a poem about anything.

Write a story. As long as you have a start, middle and end you are an author.

Write your autobiography.
Write a biography of your parents or friends.

Make up a limerick. Short and to the point, clean or smutty.

Draw something, an apple or a landscape. Paint it if you want.

Take photographs of people, events, animals, nature and landscapes.

Think of your life and your dream life as a film.

Create a video for YouTube.

Learn to play a musical instrument.

Join a drama group.

Join a choir.

Offer help to people who need it.

Create a meal for an old person or a loved one.

Key Points
Create something that makes you feel a sense of achievement.

Your creations can be for yourself or others.

9

NO MORE DISCONTENT

How to avoid and get rid of things that cause discontent.

DOMINATION CONTROL

QUEEN BEES AND HORNETS

There are people who control in the distorted name of 'love'.

There are mothers who want to live their lives through their children because their own lives were damaged. These matriarchs want to turn their daughters into models at very early ages. When I say models, that includes a physical representation of the perfect child brought up by the perfect mother (of course), or it could be a junior beauty queen (same motive) or a daughter who does not make the same mistakes in her choice of a partner so the mother inspects and rejects potential boyfriends. This control makes the children, the young adults and mature ones very unhappy and they find it hard to rebel for fear of hurting this queen bee in their lives.

If you are in this situation, please do something to make YOUR life happy. You are not a puppy to be trained in obedience; you are a free roaming creation of life. If making yourself happy makes a controller unhappy then that is a problem of their own making.

Become free, resist the emotional blackmail that is part of the control technique and learn to be the only controller of your life and happiness.

Here are men who think their children are not as good as them. They are treated as stupid and as failures. This is the father's fault, never the son or daughter.

And there are male controllers and abusers. These are men, mostly fathers, who treat their children as sex toys. You have no options other than to report this to the appropriate authorities. If you are worried that you will get into trouble because nobody will believe you, please remember that there are experts who deal with these problems and they will assure you that you are not the only person to have been abused.

The same applies to physical, verbal and emotional abuse by a male or female partner.

These are issues beyond the scope of this book but there are many sources of help available.

TRIBAL CHIEFS AT WORK

Work is where we find the tribal hierarchy that has been in existence for ever. There is a range of warriors that will be confident enough to train and help younger people to be allies and supporters for their causes.

Then there are warriors that worry that the other employees carry a threat to their position and will do what they can to pass on blame for their own mistakes. This weakens them because they lose allies and one day they will be challenged.

Warriors that worry about their place in a tribe (company) will work longer hours; will try to play political games that they will either win or lose or they will become rebels to upset the running order of the other players.

Do you remember the day you were offered your job? You went home full of pride and happy that you were needed. If you have become discontented with it then it is time to review why that original feeling changed.

If you are unhappy at work appraise your position as if you were working out a playing strategy. Nominate the characters in your game and what their roles are.

Identify what the game is about and what the winning rules are.

If you can figure out a different way to play the game, then you can find that content again. If not, then perhaps now is the time to find a different company to work for. You know your strengths and weaknesses. Use them to recover your self-belief in your values to others.

Key Points
Refuse to be dominated. It never matters who it is, your mother, father, siblings or bosses. Stand your ground. Stop abuse of any type from happening.

Job evaluation happens by bosses. Allow yourself to evaluate how you feel about your work situation. Job satisfaction is vital.

PREDATORS AND BULLIES

There might be some people who will regard you as weak because <u>they</u> are and they want to dominate to make themselves feel better. No chance.

They will have no contentment. These are predators of your emotional life and bullies of your very being and have to steal to make themselves feel better. Laugh them away.

On my walks I can watch big buzzards soaring in the sky on the wind. These can be bullies and try to predate on the young hatchlings of other birds. They are chased by magpies that resemble fighter planes chasing a big bomber. The buzzards are many times bigger than the magpies but they flap and fly hard to escape the smaller protectors. These are our role models for peace. When predators and bullies are stood up to they often run away. Using a smaller still example, watch the bully run from an angry wasp.

Be careful with physical bullies because they only know how to do damage to others but the emotional ones will give in if challenged. Remember, they are weak behind their seeming bravado.

Justice is contentment after a fashion.

Key Points
Never let bullies win. The same with predators. They are all weak and puff themselves up to appear bigger than they are. They are more miserable than most.

TAKE OFF YOUR MASK

We wear a variety of social masks that present what we want

others to see in different situations. That is fine when we it happens naturally. In fact, we are seldom aware of the different personas we show. However, when we pretend to be what we cannot live up to then we have problems.

To be is better than seeming to be. Sometimes we wear disguises that we think cover up our weaknesses and by doing so we project our insecurities onto other people. Most masks are really transparent and can be seen through.

Be the person you are, be true to yourself. If you feel the need to pretend to be a different person, then become that other person. Take on the real attributes that you are playing rather than pretend. There is an old saying that says that a good liar needs a good memory. When you become what you want to be then the truth is the only thing you have to remember.

We can pretend that we have a good life and that we have good relationships or that we are doing well at work but these are lies to other people and ourselves that will eventually become a burden.

Key Points
Be true to yourself. Throw away any masks of deception that you wear.

Become what you want to be by making an effort rather than pretending.

CRITICISM AND PRAISE

The bad is always easier to spot than the good.

Give praise where it is due. This motivates others who, in return, will respect your views and they will return good feelings to you.

Children, when they grow are not experts but praise for good efforts leads to better ones until they feel confident as young adults and thereafter.

In any relationship, personal or work-wise, praise is always more powerful and less destructive than criticism.

Words are strong and potentially destructive weapons when used badly. As a specific issue that can be generalised into different scenarios, if your partner has put on weight then telling him/her that they are fat will count against you and will build a resentment that results in even more weight gain. If you want to encourage him/her to lose weight, then offer praise for a change in eating habits or exercise regimes. Praise how good that person looked when they were slimmer without additional detail. The message is for motivation to become healthier.

In the work situation, an employee may lack motivation because their efforts are deemed to be less than they could be. Rather than criticisms and threats that they might be fired, the job of their boss is to train that person in the areas of expertise that they lack to make them more efficient. Going back to the example with children, if they cannot ride a bicycle the first few times they try, if you threaten to throw the bike away then that child will probably never learn to ride it. Praise their efforts, teach them well and they might become a Tour de France champion.

Our minds are very receptive of criticism and praise.

If you feel you have been unfairly criticised, then stand your ground calmly rather than ranting and raving. If you lose your temper, then you set yourself up for more criticism. Take a breath, think about what was said and make your case gently and without conflict.

If you are the object of unfair criticism, then ask the critic how you can change and offer praise for their help (whether you mean it or not) and they will have to explain why they have been negative to you. Play the game so they will take the praise for helping you and they will then become your ally rather than your negative judge. Devious? Who cares?

Key Points
Criticism is destructive.

Praise is motivating and always welcome.

SOCIAL MOBILITY

If you have moved into different circles in your life and have become distanced from your friends and family by geography and/or money, then you may have become discontented because your roots have become too distant.

The world has expanded and shrunk at the same time. I sometimes stay in France, forty minutes from Bordeaux airport which is an hour and fifteen minutes away from my family in England. By that, I mean that they live in very different parts of England and they are within easy reach of the four airports we can fly into.

There are telephones and Skype with which we can keep in touch. The distances from our home in England are shorter in miles but take longer to drive in terms of time to travel.

So people are within reach wherever you live but not just around the corner as they might have been a hundred years ago. We have to cope with what we have. There is a need to move for work that has to be balanced with the desire to keep in touch.

The keystone to dealing with a physical distancing of family and friends is contact.

Key Points
Keeping in touch is easy no matter how far away people are.

IMPOSING ON OTHERS

Wear metaphorical headphones!!!

Incoming
Your sense of peace can be ruined when others will not let you rest or work on your projects. They might not understand that you do not want to be disturbed so explain, ahead of what you want to do, that you would like some time on your own. Depending upon whom that person or people may be they might be suspicious of your motives. They need to know that what you are doing is decent and inoffensive. They regard their own privacy as a right, perhaps. You can say that to them in the hope that they will understand.

Then there are people who want to impose their advice on you as if you are an idiot. Change the subject. Or you could thank them for their input but explain politely that you have thought the matter through and you have come to you own conclusions.

Outgoing
Never impose your tastes on others who do not wish to share them. These include sensitive topics such as sex, food, music, art, TV programmes, religion, politics and so on.

If these topics arise then you can listen and comment but avoid preaching your viewpoint to others. See the effect in the 'incoming' section above. You will alienate people who do not have the same ideas about contentious issues as yourself. You can discuss and debate them but never become a bigot with fixed opinions within a closed mind.

To close the metaphor above, wear metaphorical headphone and turn off your loudspeakers. Listen and broadcast at a comfortable volume.

Key Points
Stop people from imposing their presence or views on you.

Avoid imposing your presence or views on other people. Be able to calmly discuss topics.

AVOID

Avoid things in your life that are judgemental.

Television is full of trivial competitions that place ranks on skills and performance. Talent shows will show the poor but 'amusing' entrants because it fills space and makes people laugh at others. The socially inept people who appeared on programmes such as the now defunct Jeremy Kyle's are there to make the audience laugh at the problems of others whilst feeling good that the viewers are 'better' than the exhibits in the freak show.

Quiz shows can hurt us because the knowledge that we have does not win us the huge amounts of prize money on offer.

Politicians bitch at each other and talk in terms of the other person's failure to bring miracles about. Contentment is not on their agenda. Discontent with their competition by the voters is what they need to win ballots.

It suggests that failure is normal.

The bottom line is that we become surrounded by negativity which sucks our contentment away.

Key Points
Avoid being immersed in negativity when possible because it sets a low standard for our lives.

PROCRASTINATION

Stop making excuses for not doing something. Do it and the problem disappears.

Make lists of the things you have to do and tackle the least desirable one first. After that do the second thing and so on. Having done the jobs that you least like then your, motivation to do the rest will increase.

When your chores are up to date you will gain a sense of satisfaction.

In short, make a start with <u>SOMETHING</u> and enjoy the sense of fulfilment when you have finished. Hopefully somebody will notice and offer praise. If they do not, then point out your achievement and feel good.

Key Points
"My advice is to never do tomorrow what you can do today. Procrastination is the thief of time." Charles Dickens

10

BALANCING YOUR LIFE

Is resolution of the balance of one or some of the following at the base of your lack of self-belief?

Rather than skip through the A to Z lists on the following pages decide how each point might influence you and see if you can resolve some of your issues.

NOT ENOUGH:

Acknowledgement

When you make an effort for others either at work or in your private life it is good that you are acknowledged. Being taken for granted is hurtful and leads to bitterness which is the opposite of contentment. If your labours are worthy but unrecognised, then bring it to the attention of the person who lacks the politeness to notice. If that upsets them then it is sad but you are the person who has made the effort. If you are a grandparent who offered to child mind the grandchildren make sure it is known that it is a favour rather than a full-time job. It is within your time for yourself and that might include childminding but you have other things in your life which you should not stop because you feel committed to doing your offspring a kindness.

Balance

Do you give too much for no return? Do you receive too little from others? Balance is about equals on both sides.

Communicate your concerns and discuss your needs to make your life and the other person's life a happy and stable combination.

Compliments

Rather than looking for glowing praise for your work or appearance you can expect kind words for the way you are. If you give compliments then, very often, you will receive them in return. You can establish a culture of well-being that will be self-sustaining. Compare this with the example of a culture of insults where people will go to great lengths to create bad feelings when upset. They are verbal bullies. They feel better because they have become involved in a power game. If that can be applied to tributes, then we will enjoy life better.

Contact

We are conceived from close contact and we grow up with it for food, love and social development. It is within our genes that we should seek out people, friends and family for company. Talk to others face to face, write, phone or Skype depending on proximity. They have as much need for contact as you do.

Love

'Let us always meet each other with smile, for the smile is the beginning of love.' Mother Teresa.

'Love isn't something you find. Love is something that finds you.' Loretta Young

Whether you have lost love or you are seeking for it to grow or for it to come into your life, those two quotes sum up what is needed. You should put on a happy smile to face the world and then people will see in you what they are seeking, a person to be at peace with and to share their feelings. Dream of love in your life and it will change your attitude towards others. They need to feel comfortable with you.

Money

There are two solutions, earn more and/or spend less. Earning more can be difficult in these lean times but if you feel comfortable in asking for a pay rise, do so. Changing jobs is an easy thing to say but difficult in reality. However, keep your eyes and ears open for opportunities. If you do not, then you will miss any chances that are available.

As for spending less it is a good idea to audit your outgoings. You can make small changes and those can add up to substantial amounts. For example, check your fridge to see how much you overbuy and throw away. Sometime two-for-one offers seem like value but are you consuming what you have bought? It is a good idea to think of your meal menus for the week and buy only the things you need for them. A good tip is to go to the supermarket on a full stomach because it reduces the urge for impulse buying. Other things you can do include walking or cycling more so that you drive less and spend a smaller amount of money on fuel. Adjust your heating in winter to a lower level and wear warmer clothes.

It is only when you check on your spending that you can make those little savings that will add up.

Sex

If your partner has a very different sex drive to you then you need to seek a balance of needs by discussing what you both want as a solution. If this does not suit your partner or you and you cannot reach agreement, then the problem will remain. Perhaps you will both need to seek help from a professional source but there will be a smattering of resentment from both of you. Agreement is easy if the love in the relationship is strong enough.

Time

Organise. Cut back on unnecessary usage of time. For example, clean the house less often. Nobody will notice anyway. Time can be made.

Likewise, with work ensure that you have equilibrium with the hours you spend earning your pay with the time you spend with your family and friends.

Material gains are made worthless after emotional losses. If balance is kept then the search for wealth is fine but when the happiness of those people who you love and who love you is damaged, it becomes the real price, and then all the wealth in the world will never repair it?

AntiSocial Media

Social media sometimes get a bad press. It is implied that the Internet connections inhibit 'real' friendships, they make you isolated and so on. But if you are isolated, have no friends and have no contacts then you can get these from your social media pages.

After all they are so popular because lots of people use them. Life is not usually full of meeting strangers in the shopping mall with whom you can have a conversation. Places to meet people in 'real' life are fraught with the same dangers as the internet. However, there are sharks who want you for their own pleasure.

If you need contact with people or you wish to meet folk with similar interests, then use social media.

Always be wary of people you meet either in a public place or on the Internet, but having said that, you can, if you are careful, find folk to share interests with.

Bear in mind that, sadly, social media attracts some weirdos who want to stalk, bully and insult others. If that happens, take action. Close them down and/or call the police.

Key Points
Use social media if you find making face to face friends difficult.

Be careful when contacting strangers. Some are not what they seem to be.

Poison Pens and Fingers
In the past, poison pen letters were written to insult and upset the readers. Based mostly on gossip, they were malicious and cruel. Messages on phones, android devices and laptops and social media can have the same effect.

The danger is when she/he will not do or say what you want her/him to do or say so then you get angry and say things or send messages that are nasty and hurtful.

This makes her/him even less likely to do or say the things you would like her/him to do or say, and so you get angrier still.

The cycle goes on until everything that was good gets smothered and then breaks.

The only solution is to break the cycle. You cannot change her/him. The only person you can change is yourself.

Alcohol is a depressant and you can become angry for no logical reason after drinking a lot. It is as if alcohol blocks the critical ability to restrict negative feelings. These are often irrational and can be based on jealousy, resentment and failure to control the other person.

The best advice is to turn off any device that you might use to damage your relationship and keep quiet. The added benefit is that the person who you might be rude to when drunk will be unable to contact you. If they did then you will be back at square one.

If you have ever written messages that you regretted even once, learn from this, never do it again and take measures to prevent it happening. Never rely upon the drunken mind of your Dummy to be sensible.

Words That Hurt
Sticks and stones may break my bones but words will never hurt me.

Maybe in terms of physical hurts that heal, sticks and stones will hurt but in terms of emotional scarring, words are a lethal weapon. The damage they can cause will last a lifetime. Insults and accusations work their way into a person's mind like a burrowing parasite, consuming love and eating away at any feelings of warmth the recipient had.

One thing to bear in mind is:
Always have awareness of your words and actions and their potential consequences. Destroying is easy, building is hard.

You are reading this perhaps, because you have hurt somebody or have been hurt. Word violence can lead to physical violence either as a continuation of an onslaught or as a defence. Neither is acceptable and should be avoided. Think before you speak.

A Four Letter Word Beginning with C
There is a four-letter word that begins with the letter C. It is a bad word and a good word depending on how it is used.

The word is care. There are people who make mistakes because they care. They were trying their utmost to help themselves and others but something went wrong in their efforts. At least they attempted to improve.

And then there are people who make mistakes because they have no care. They want something for themselves at the expense of others. 'Who cares?'

When you want to recycle your emotions and your baggage, you should be doing it for the peace and tranquillity of others around you, the people you love and would like to be loved by. Their state of emotional well-being will reflect upon you. The desire for change must be for the concern of those around you as well as yourself. These are simple laws of nature; what goes around comes around and the other is reap what you shall sow. All actions, verbal or physical have consequences and repercussions.

Those people who make mistakes because they care will feel the reflection of their good intent shine back on them.

Those who lack care will be seen by others as people who deserve what they get.

Forget Divine intervention; it is something held in human nature. In our early caveman days, those hunters who cared for others shared their meat. They were seen as valuable members of the tribe. Those who gave nothing to others were the last to be given food when times were hard.

We all make mistakes but some follow a lack of care and others are from being caring. Be one of the good folk.

If you have made mistakes because you care, then please accept the guidance given to put those errors behind you and move forward.

11

CONFIDENCE AND SELF-ESTEEM

Belief in yourself and your abilities is important. When you feel good about who you are and what you are able to do, you grow. How to start to build confidence when you believe that you lack it is a challenge, but run a check on what you have in your favour. Be like Superman. He was a weakling in his normal life, Clark Kent, but a superhero when he had to be. Identify which qualities you have that make you feel you are like Clark. Write them down. Then imagine what you would be like as Superman, the strengths you would have in talking to others, working, showing that super confidence. Change the original you into the super-you and then throw away the old you and block the way to return. Stand taller, straighter. Walk as if the world relied on you; talk as if you were a guru with faith in your words. Do this from this moment and, like magic, as long as you adopt the persona of the kind, confident and successful person you would like to be, then that is what you will become.

If you want to meet and talk to other people but you are shy, watch good conversationalists and copy what they do and how they do it. See how they hold their bodies, their faces and how they move to others to start talking. You will notice that seemingly good talkers are actually very good at asking questions and then listening to the answers. They lead talk rather than make talk. Examples are:

"How are you?"

"What do you do for a living?"
"What are your hobbies?"
"What do you think about the headlines?"

These are leading questions that need an explanatory answer rather than simple questions such as "Do you like opera?" that require nothing more than a 'yes' or 'no' answer.

When you get responses then your confidence grows. The input is small for the results you achieve.

Develop empathy. Put yourself inside the other person's head. Ask yourself how much they understand about what you talking about

Selling benefits is more than something that is used for products. "I would like a job in your company, please." Says nothing. "I am a person with experience of making profits in your industry and I am able to apply those skills instantly." Gets interest. The person you are talking to is more interested in increasing profits rather than you as a human being and your confidence shines through. Once that person realises that you are able to benefit the company, then they will be interested in you.

Write down your benefits to other people, to businesses, to the arts, to person-kind and whichever other categories you can. I know already that you will hit walls. "I am of no use to anybody!" Oh yes you are. Start again and again until you have a big list. Copy the attributes of others, find similarities. Hey, celebrities have little use other than being celebrities. So why do we have them? They must have some use, surely!

So, what does this achieve? It increases your feeling of self-worth. It builds confidence. People who lack confidence need to discover the gems that they are that are covered in dirt. That is you. Find your inner qualities and resources.

Be assertive (rather than aggressive). Compare "Do you have a reservation for me for dinner, please? My name is Jones." with "Hello. My name is Jones. You have a reservation for me this evening." Said to a restaurant waiter the second makes a statement rather than asking a question that requires a 'yes' or 'no' answer. If the restaurant is overbooked then you will lose it in the first instance and get in the second. Build assertion into your speech to avoid people taking advantage of you.

So, set your goals, develop the skills and the role model to achieve them. Find your personal assets and build on them. Just go for it but make sure it is legal!

Being aware of your skills will allow others to recognise those talents. For example, in my days as a hypnotherapist, very few people asked if I could hypnotise. The vast majority knew that I could by my job title and allowed themselves to be relaxed. We expect dentists to treat our teeth and doctors to sort our health problems. They demonstrate their confidence in what they do.

I had a short operation to remove an old root below a dental crown. It was quick, easy and painless. When I complimented the dental surgeon, he just replied that it was his metier, his profession, so what should I have expected. He smiled as he spoke.

Confidence, self-belief and esteem come from you knowing that what you do is done to the best level of skill and dedication you have. Being proud is never a sin. It is something good and constructive that should be absorbed into our feeling of being the best.

Lack of confidence can come from a fear of being criticised. That is only valid if the critics are perfect. Theatre critics are never always good playwrights, nor food critics good chefs. Their job is to criticise skills in others that thy lack themselves.

It is worth thinking about winners in sport, business and entertainment. None of them were born as champions, they had to learn their skills step by step, day by day. Expecting to be super confident in a miraculous moment is a big wish. But follow the ways they did it. They honed their talents, some with the help of trainers, by spotting weaknesses and then correcting them to improve. It is always a process until you reach the point when you know you have what you dreamed of.

Take your confidence building like you are climbing the rungs of a ladder. Go higher, congratulate yourself, and go higher still. If your feet slip, explore why it happened and take action to prevent it happening again.

Then the day will arrive when you can say, as Muhammad Ali did, 'I am the greatest.'

12

THE ART OF CALM

Some of the following points have been touched on already but remember the expert public speakers who say, 'Tell them what you are going to say, then tell what you have to say, and then tell them what you have just told them.'

Repetition is deliberate in order to emphasize key issues that make the difference we desire because they are better absorbed.

BREATHING

Learning how to breathe correctly is very important. In this way you give yourself a way to relax and a way to cope.

In history, breathing was considered to be such an important part of life that the word 'spirit' comes from 'spiritus', the Latin word for breath, as in respiration. It is also the root word for inspiration. However, it is one of the things that is often overlooked, or misunderstood. The effect of the breath is at the very heart of problems and, happily, solutions.

Breathing in the correct way has been taught for centuries. To the Yogis of India, the word 'prana' means the element to which all other substances might finally be reduced as is the spirit of life in Western culture. Regulation of the breath is known as 'pranayama' and it is practised for mental and physical wellbeing.

In China, the same thing is known as 'Chi', as in Tai Chi, a routine of slow meditative physical exercise for relaxation and balance and health. In other words, the practice and benefits of breathing correctly have been known for thousands of years for spiritual (mental) and bodily well-being. However, modern culture has dictated that we should have body shapes that emphasise the chest and minimize the stomach. That is the very shape that inhibits correct breathing.

We breathe from the moment that we are born so we feel that we know how to do it correctly. And we do. After all, we are alive! As a point of interest, when we die, we expire! I get looks of surprise when I talk to people about the correct ways to breathe.

The lungs are misunderstood! We tend to think of them as a pair of balloon-like bags in our chests that take oxygen in and push carbon dioxide out. They are, in fact, complex excretory organs. They are made from tubes and cavities that allow the exchange of gases. They remove many waste products as well as carbon dioxide, which is why we can smell garlic on people's breath. The little cavities, called alveoli, work constantly and are independent of the respiratory, or breathing, cycle. The process of gas exchange is dependent upon their concentrations. Waste gases either remain in the lungs until flushed out by breathing or are re-absorbed into the bloodstream when the concentration increases. The re-absorption of those exhaust gases can make people feel anxious, uncomfortable, nervous and irritable. The breathing rate is controlled by blood acidity levels so an increase in carbon dioxide in the blood stream increases carbonic acid levels. This, in turn, increases the rate at which we breathe to eliminate excesses of carbon dioxide to achieve a natural balance. However, hyperventilation occurs when carbon dioxide, and carbonic acid levels fall too low, which constricts the blood vessels restricting blood flow to the brain.

Sufferers from panic attacks are often told to take deep breaths to prevent hyperventilation. However, the instructions about how to do this are often very often counter-productive. Some experts appear to misunderstand what they instructing their clients or patients to do!

We are taught from an early age that neatness is important in body posture. If you take a deep breath, as you were instructed by their parents, schoolteachers and others whose intentions are to produce that neatness, then you will probably breathe into the high chest. This produces tension and stiffness in the neck and shoulder muscles, and a drawing in of the stomach.

If you simulate the position that you would adopt under attack, it is the same. The neck and shoulders tighten to protect the throat and the back of the head. The stomach muscles tighten to protect the soft organs of the abdomen, the liver, kidneys and spleen from injury. The legs cross to protect the genitals.

In this way, poor advice to breathe deeply actually imitates the posture of somebody under threat. Remember that panic, anxiety, stress and anger are responses to a threat, whether real or imaginary. It is important to breathe deeply into the abdomen rather than the high chest. In this way you will signal to your mind that you are safe, and thereby evoke a recovery response that counters those feelings of anxiety. Breathing involves two sets of muscles.

The intercostal muscles.

These extend downwards and connect the ribs. When they are contracted the ribs are pulled upwards and outwards to enlarge the rib cage (thoracic cavity). These are the breathing muscles that predominate during the anxiety state when the blood needs to be well oxygenated. They can work rapidly to produce panting which can lead to hyperventilation where the blood is over oxygenated and leads to tingling in the extremities of the body and light-headedness. This accounts for the high number of panic attack victims who are admitted to the cardio-vascular units of hospitals.

The diaphragm.

This is a dome shaped muscle at the base of the lungs. When contracted it 'flattens' and it causes air to flow into the lungs. Its effect is to enlarge the thoracic cavity in length. The diaphragm is the muscle that sucks air into the lower parts of the lungs and in turn, it flushes out waste gases that collect there. This type of breathing is indicative of a relaxed state. It is the natural way to breathe. Every child breathes in this way until school age.

Breathing, theoretically, includes the use of both sets of muscles to ensure an entrance of fresh air and the expulsion of waste products throughout the lungs. The high-chest breathing which occurs during anxiety states involves the use of the intercostal muscles and the locking of the diaphragm as a result of taught stomach muscles.

The exercises that follow will encourage you to use your diaphragm as the main muscle for respiration.

4 x 4 BREATHING

STARTING POSITION Lie on your back on the floor. Make sure that you are safe to do so. Pick up a medium sized book to put over your stomach just at the point where the rib cage ends. Ensure that your neck and shoulder muscles are loose and relaxed. Relax your stomach muscles.	**START**
STEP ONE Breathe deeply into your stomach to raise the book as if you were trying to lift it to touch the ceiling for the duration of your slow count of four. Keep your chest as still as possible.	**LIFT** 1...2...3...4 (Please note: Whilst breathing in, avoid inflating the upper parts of your lungs because they will fill automatically.)
STEP TWO Hold the book, in the raised position, for your slow count of four of the same duration as in step one.	**HOLD** 1...2...3...4
STEP THREE Breathe out to lower the book for the same count of four. Imagine that you are lowering it to touch your backbone.	**DOWN** 1...2...3...4

STEP FOUR	LEAVE ON BACKBONE
Then leave your lungs feeling 'empty' for a count of four.	1...2...3...4 

As we are conditioned to breathe with the high chest, concentrating on using the diaphragm will result in a balanced breathing practice. The above, the 4 x 4 Breathing Method, is a superb exercise to learn.

IF YOU HAVE MEDICAL PROBLEMS, THEN BEFORE DOING THE EXERCISES. YOU SHOULD CONSULT YOUR DOCTOR. THIS REFERS TO THE BACK, KNEES AND JOINTS AS WELL AS THE LUNGS.

There are three benefits to doing this exercise.

1 The fight or flight response is caused by a part of the mind that is beyond conscious control. There is an opposing system also beyond conscious control that can be tricked into operation. Because you are laying on the floor you might feel slightly vulnerable. This vulnerability in a controlled situation is reminiscent of the cave dweller being in a safe place after being chased by a predator. The body needed to come down to a state where energy consumption was low and where repairs could take place. When relaxed the immune system is maximised. The position you are in replicates those circumstances and the relaxation response (the parasympathetic branch of the autonomic nervous system) kicks in.

2 The exercise strengthens the diaphragm. This is a big muscle that weakens when underused. When it flattens out it also

massages the gut from above, aiding digestion. This means that, with the increased levels of relaxation, this has a double benefit for sufferers from anxiety and IBS.

3 Whilst concentrating on breathing in a fairly unusual way, your mind will be distracted from the worries that caused you to be tense.

As a species we are vulnerable at four points on the body. They are the back of the neck, the throat, the soft abdominal organs (liver, kidneys, spleen etc.) and our genitals. The above exercise exposes them. (A horribly ambiguous word that, in this case, means in a covered and decent way.)

CATS AND DOGS

Observe your pets if you have any, or those belonging to friends and family. They know how to breathe because they do it naturally without regard to the fashionable appearance of their bodies. When relaxed and safe they use the diaphragm to breathe. When they are running you will notice rapid, high-chest breathing. If they say "walkies" to their sleeping dogs, which is heard in dog language as 'let's go hunting', the diaphragmatic breathing will immediately change to panting. The dog is increasing the oxygen in its bloodstream in order to be ready for action.

Every animal on this planet breathes correctly apart from the human who lives in our modern culture. The desire for big chests and flat stomachs has caused modern society to adopt the breathing patterns that promote anxiety and stress disorders.

EXASPERATION!

When we are irritated by something, we often take a deep breath in, hold it and then breathe out with a sigh of exasperation. This is a natural phenomenon that, in our primeval days, took us from a high-energy state to a recovery state in brief moments. We can use this response without being irritated. It is similar in effect to the 'explosive relaxation' technique described later, but with a focus on breathing rather than posture.

OPERA SINGERS AND SWIMMERS

An opera singer has to be able to sing long complicated word structures as well as high, low and long notes.

Like a swimmer, the opera singer has to master breathing. Whereas it is difficult to imitate the swimmer's breathing patterns, it is easier to play a charade as an opera singer!

Encourage yourself to take deep breaths and pretend to sing long notes. This should be done in private rather than in your office! This helps to automatically use both the intercostal and diaphragmatic muscles.

In TV talent shows the singing coaches will concentrate on diaphragmatic breathing, I am sure. This helps the singer to sing AND to relax in what could be one of the most stress causing scenarios that we can imagine.

A quick tip, breathe as if you are inhaling and exhaling through your belly button. This focuses your mind on abdominal breathing.

POSTURE

When we feel fearful or aggressive, our bodies tighten. Just as there is communication between our minds and our bodies, there is interaction between our body positions and our emotions. When we adopt certain positions, we tell our minds that there is a potential 'alert state', and our mental processes react accordingly. This is fairly obvious when it involves negative effects, but the body/mind relationship can be used in a positive way in order to mediate the fight or flight response.

We are very similar to chimpanzees, gorillas and orang-utans, yet none of them stand to attention or sit up straight, apart from us humans. Only we have to eat with our elbows off the table!

Our body postures relate to our feelings of well-being. There are two phrases, which exemplify this connection between body attitude and state of mind, 'up-tight' and 'laid-back'.

When we are tense, nervous or anxious our bodies tighten up. This is because we are in the early stages of the fight or flight response. We feel under threat from something that is outside ourselves or from that feeling of dread that can grow from our minds. The closing up of our bodies protects us, to some extent, when under physical threat.

To feel how our muscles are linked when under attack, do the following. Relax your neck, shoulder and stomach muscles. Now tighten your stomach muscles. Notice how your neck and shoulders tighten in sympathy. You can do it the other way around. There is no direct connection between the muscles, but the signals from one part of your body are transmitted through your mind to the other.

The same thing happens when you extend an arm and make a tight fist. The tension is felt all the way up to the neck.

When our bodies become tense, our minds read the signs and start to worry about what the assumed threat might be. Think about the body positions of anxiety sufferers even when they are in a safe place. Likewise, the people who have been bullied will sink their heads into the shoulders. The stomach muscles are firmed. The legs and arms are crossed. All without reason. We could understand the body posture if the victim were surrounded by thugs, but even when secure, the body reflects the possibility of being attacked. We can use the body to persuade the mind that there is no need to panic, that the best response is to relax and recover, to be 'laid-back'.

The significance of an awareness of body position and muscle tone in controlling anxiety is that when the body feels prepared for an assumed attack then the mind is involved and sets the fight or flight response into motion. Tension in the body promotes tension in the mind.

The contrary applies, however. When the body is relaxed, it signals to the mind that it is safe and the recovery response kicks in. We can consciously control the positions and tension of our muscles; therefore, we actually have conscious control of the recovery response, albeit in an indirect way. We trick the system that is supposed to be beyond conscious control into action.

As written earlier, we are no more than primeval animals in modern dress. We still live in the pattern of our ancient ancestors. There are situations in our lives that remind us, at some level, of our earlier days and we respond accordingly.

In a society where food is fairly abundant it is difficult to imagine how we must have been when dividing the spoils of a hunt. Yet we watch hyenas and lions snarling at, and biting each other in wildlife documentaries on TV. We see animals fighting off rivals in the mating process. We were like that, so it will come as no surprise that we become tense and anxious in social situations that involve food and courtship.

I have seen many people who were distressed when eating in restaurants, or who were unable to swallow their meals. This unconscious worry about the possible aggression of others can lie at the heart of the panicking supermarket shopper where we 'take' self-service food, which we feel others want. It is different in a small store where we are served. Our ancestors would have felt comfortable when handed food, without risk, by the elders after they had first taken their fill.

We observe the bullying which takes place in schools as children play domination and submission roles. We see the worries that some people have in crowds where others are seen as unfriendly and frightening. The work situation is often difficult to cope with when colleagues and bosses are reflecting early social hostilities. Stress is more often caused by people in the workplace rather than by the work itself.

When we feel threats that are real or implied, then we close our bodies to protect our existence. Our muscles tighten and our minds race. This is the fight-or-flight response in action. Release the tension, open your body and signal your mind to calm down.

When you do this, you relax because you stimulate the recovery response into action.

It is useful to watch pets when they are resting. They will sleep in a very exposed position when feeling safe and secure. Children, before being told how to sit like adults, will relax on the floor in front of the television. This is our natural and instinctive positioning until we are made to change to conform to adult standards of order. So copy children and pets. Learn from them. Lounge around and be casual. Then you will feel more relaxed. Learn to be calm and comfortable, or 'laid-back'.

EXPLOSIVE RELAXATION

This exercise teaches us to recognise that instant relief is possible when we are feeling tense. Take an UP-TIGHT position and suddenly explode into the exposed position shown in the 'BE LAID-BACK' frame below. All tension disperses instantly and you will receive a sense of peace. You can enhance this feeling with slow and deep abdominal breathing, described in the breathing section.

Here is how you do it:

Sit on an armchair or comfortable couch. Make sure it is sturdy enough to take your body weight when you flop backwards.

Tighten your muscles to adopt a rigid body position. Place the hands together palm to palm. Then pull your feet back, close to the chair. Then close your eyes and adopt the 'up-tight' position.

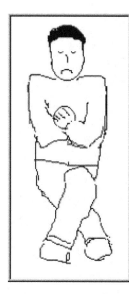

UP-TIGHT

This body position represents hiding from the environment, which includes people as well as animals and physical objects. We focus our vision into a stare (or close our eyes), tighten our muscles and protect ourselves.

When we sit in this 'up-tight' position our mind fears an attack and we become predisposed to anxiety or panic. The fear of anxiety or panic makes us even more tense, and so on.

Take a deep breath into your stomach and hold it.

In your mind, you count from 3 down to 1, and say, to yourself, the word "NOW."
Then should sprawl out. Your head goes back to the chair or couch. Your legs part in front of you by 18 inches or so as they make contact with the floor with your heels. Your arms fly out to the side, palms upwards.

As you relax there you can breathe gently through your navel. You are now 'laid-back'.

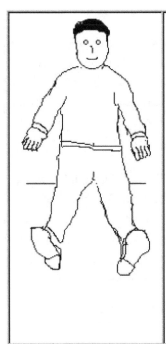

BE LAID-BACK

You 'expose' yourself to the environment. This opens up the paths for relaxed, diaphragmatic breathing.

This signals to your mind that your body is safe from threat. Your mind will perceive this and bring the recovery response into play which allows you to relax even more.

This is the positive feedback that your mind and body needs in order to find relief from panic, anxiety, stress and anger.

You may have recognised that this position is very similar to that adopted by practitioners of meditation, the difference being that the calves of your legs are stretched outwards rather than the legs being bent at the knees in the lotus position. You will have taught yourself how to relax in a similar way to the way the Beatles did in India, but in a shorter space of time.

ENSURE THAT YOU AVOID THE FOLLOWING:

1. Ankle crossing.

When at work, commuting or eating in restaurants, watch other people. The vast majority will have their legs crossed at the ankles with their feet tucked back below their knees. This is a sign of tension. It causes the leg muscles to tense and this is fed back to their minds. You should uncross your ankles and extend your feet forwards onto your heels. You should breathe using your diaphragm.

2. Badly set-up computer keyboards.

If you use a keyboard or laptop, review the position that you adopt when typing. Very often, screen angles will cause the neck to bend backwards which duplicates the 'under threat' position. Some people in open plan offices feel vulnerable when they have their backs to their colleagues. They should change orientation if this is a problem.

3. Dehydration.

Dehydration, such as that which follows drinking alcohol or large quantities of coffee, makes people feel anxious. Many people report having their first anxiety attack after drinking alcohol heavily during the previous evening. The solution for them is to avoid excess alcohol, to reduce coffee intake and/or to drink plenty of water.

4. Feeling trapped.

Feelings of being trapped are felt in a variety of situations including crowds, restaurants, cinemas, theatres, supermarkets, trains, aircraft and when driving. Techniques for changing language, posture and breathing practices are key factors in controlling the fight or flight response that follows exposure to the situation or feared object. Encourage yourself to know and to believe that you are in control.

5. Food competition.

This has a primeval connection. Food has been such an important factor of life since history began that we become competitive in any situation where there is social interaction involving food. This includes restaurants and self-service stores and supermarkets. Even the check-out, the place where some people feel like rushing away, is the point which represents losing the product of the hunt to scavengers. In these situations, people should remember that they are free of dissension over foodstuffs. There is plenty to go around. So much, in fact, that what we see on our plates or in our trolleys is always non-contentious, so they are safe.

6. Gripping.

There are specific situations where gripping an object can make people feel anxious. The tension of a vice-like grip tightens the muscles in the neck and shoulders. Then the stomach tenses and the body goes into an amber alert. From there, anything can happen!

The common scenarios are the following:

The steering wheel.

When driving, you should hold the steering wheel gently as if holding the wrists of a baby. They must maintain control, obviously, but without clenching.

The pram handle.

Again, the you can maintain control, but with a looser grip.

The supermarket trolley handle.

If your load is heavy, a supermarket trolley can become difficult to control, so you must either shop more frequently, although this can become a nuisance and adds to anxiety, or, better still, you can ask your partner to push the trolley! Just loosening the grip helps.

The golf club.
Gripping too tightly can cause enough tension to upset the swings of golfers. Another result is something called 'the yips', the inability to hit a putt on the green. If these are problems for you then you should loosen the grip, breathe with the diaphragm, and above all, just enjoy a game that is supposed to be a pleasure.

7. Holding a newspaper in the air.
As with a steering wheel, holding a newspaper can tighten the neck and shoulders, bringing about a feeling of anxiety. Look at the stressed faces of commuting business people. When they get to their offices, they are feeling either timid or aggressive.

8. Hunching.
Anxious people hunch in many different situations. These include meeting others socially, being interviewed, sitting in restaurants, driving, working and sitting at home. They can be shown that they can stand or sit without tightening the neck, shoulders and stomach. As well as looking more relaxed, they will feel it.

9. Sexual/Social competition.
This is another point of primeval worry. Anxiety, jealousy and anger come from the fear that we might be attacked or have our mate stolen from us. This is most easily seen in places where teenagers and singles meet. In these situations, it is better to be with friends who offer security of numbers or to avoid places which have a reputation for trouble.

For mothers on a school run there is sometimes a worry about how others will regard their competence as mothers. You must learn that your child is the best in the world and that you are the person who raised him/her. Therefore, you are the best mum, ever.

10. Wearing a collar and tie too tightly.

Fashion works against us society. The brain needs a large amount of blood flowing through it. If we wear ties too tightly, or if collars are too small for our necks, then neckwear becomes a garrotte rather than clothing. A tight collar will also put pressure on the neck muscles so that you might tighten them to counteract the noose. This encourages neck and shoulder muscles to contract which, as we know, stimulates anxiety.

Where possible, anxious people should leave their ties off, or loosen them. This might go against the grain for an anxious person but with a looser collar they should become less anxious and they should also look at our business leaders like Richard Branson and successful men such as Simon Cowell. They rarely, if ever, wear ties.

13
PUTTING IT ALL TOGETHER

We need to train our minds to be free of our old behaviours and ways of thinking that hold us back from being able to be happy.

When you were a child you used to use nappies or diapers for your personal waste. Then the time came when you were 'trained' to use a potty.

Then you outgrew that and learnt to use a toilet. You have no need for any of those aids now. You have grown up and they have been dispensed with.

If you get my drift, when you still use childhood tactics to get your own way by shouting, screaming, being vile and having tantrums they hold as much use in your life now as the nappy and potty have.

You were trained to use those childhood things and then you were trained to use what adults use and they became things of the past.

In the same way, you can train your mind to dispose of those childish behaviours and learn to live a free and happy life.

So how do we do this?

In the last section you were shown how to breathe to relax, you were shown how to change your posture and earlier the words you use to bring about change.

Here is an exercise that will help you to put everything together and move into your future from this point on.

YOUR PERSONAL SOAP OPERA:

You are going to be the scriptwriter of your own soap opera. Soaps are based on the idea that life is imperfect. There are murders, rapes, bad relationships, infidelity, jealousy and so on. You name it, if it is bad, it will be in there. The women are usually good looking and the men handsome. This does not reflect reality; it is a story cobbled together to encourage people to watch and the cliff hangers that you get appeal to curiosity. They were originally created to sell detergents using advertisements to get to the listeners and viewers. Now there is always a ranking war between television channels and soaps rate high in viewing figures.

So why is this relevant to you?

You are going to become the creator of your own soap but the difference is that it is about being happy. Rather than people being nasty, you will add in friends, real or imaginary, who are nice, they are pleasant. Your story is about being contented. You can add a part where you explain that once you were troubled by disruptive behaviours and miserable relations, but NOW, you are cheery and jovial. Your soap would not bring a huge audience that thrives on misery but, you can be the only viewer because it does not matter to you that the voyeurs of malice avoid your wonderful and pleasing story. There nothing preventing you from writing it down or sharing it with a friend.

So now sit in a comfortable place, there are no rules here, just make yourself comfortable in the 'laid back' position shown above.

Breathe gently into your diaphragm as if you were breathing by using your navel, remember.

Now tell your story using the structure of words explained above. You had a problem with whatever or whoever, BUT NOW you are calm, in control and happy.

14

ANGER MANAGEMENT

ANGER IS A CAUSE OF LOSS OF SELF-BELIEF.

ANGER DESTROYS LIVES. It destroys relationships. Rather than learning how to live with your anger you must learn how to get rid of it.

Anger is an outcome of the fight or flight response. It is potentially the most dangerous inheritance from our primeval past. Back then we had to protect ourselves from predators, including other humans. We had to hunt for, and kill, our prey. We had to use adrenaline to run faster, punch harder and frighten away those creatures we were too weak to defend against.

In our more recent history, the war cry, the threatening gestures in battle and the intended intimidation of others was vital to staying alive. How inappropriate those things have become in a bar, in an office or at home!

Anger is often an expression of frustration that is misdirected at others. We might become angry with our boss and because we are worried that we could lose our jobs, we can take that anger out on our families. This vents our frustrations but causes bigger problems that in their turn create more anger.

The process of displacement, or misdirection, is a difficult one to describe but an example serves better. A man who becomes

149

angry with his wife might just be uttering feelings that he developed as a child towards his mother but was too small to express them. When he grows into the position of having a partner who, for whatever reason, reminds him of his childhood, then that bottled up rage detonates and hurts the person he loves the most. This never justifies the anger but shows that it is often inappropriate and totally out of place. Nor does it suggest in any way that the man should become angry with his mother. As a mature person he needs to understand what happened in his childhood and come to terms with his life as it is in the present day. All he needs, like everybody else, is love and to be seen in a positive light. That never comes from expressing himself in an angry, violent or verbally abusive way.

We have to become used to living in a society that uses different laws to those of the fang and claw if we want to be happy.

Anger can be dealt with by tackling a great number of areas. If anger is a major outcome of your fight or flight response then:

AVOID

Alcohol

Avoid alcohol if this relates to your anger. Drinking to excess has become a part of modern life. It helps people to lose inhibitions or, in other words, lose control of social customs that have enabled us to live together in small social spaces. Fifty thousand years ago there was a lot of space. Now we are cramped together in towns, cities and on motorways. When people drink and lose control there is a temptation to express those frustrations on the nearest person physically or emotionally.

Judging other people.

Avoid judging other people. Again, because we lack space, we form opinions about others and we assume that we know their value. We rarely do.

Carrying grudges.

Avoid carrying grudges. We want to seek revenge for assumed wrongs. Back in time, if a bear killed our friends then we wanted to seek revenge by killing the bear. That had a survival value. Carrying a grudge against other people never helps life to continue in today's society.

Working out a response

Avoid working out a response to a comment before listening and understanding the other person's point of view.

Assuming

Avoid assuming that you know what the other person is thinking. Unless we are psychic, we never know what the other person is thinking. We need to listen to find out. As once said "To assume makes an ASS out of U and ME."

Jeopardising your future

Avoid jeopardising your future by being rash and out of control. A punch thrown at somebody WILL change your life for the worse. Calling your partner foul names will have a negative effect on your relationship that time is unable to heal. Screaming at your boss will get you fired.

Lecturing to make a point.

Avoid lecturing to make a point. This is where you only want to talk rather than listen. When you lecture other people, you look and sound like a fool rather than a professor.

Being determined to change the other person's point of view to yours.
Avoid being determined to change the other person's point of view to yours. You are aggressively telling the other person why you are right and they are wrong. Are you always right? No! Sometimes you think you are, though! Listen to what the other person is saying and if you disagree, then 'beg to differ'.

Being self-absorbed.
Avoid being self-absorbed. You are likely to behave like a small child having a tantrum because you are not getting your way. Act like an adult as an alternative.

INSTEAD

Listen
Listen to the content of the conversation rather than the noise. Understand and comprehend what is being said.

Consider
Consider the longer-term implications of angry outbursts. Divorce, jail or job loss?

Learn to release feelings safely.
Vent your anger by throwing slices of bread to (never at) the ducks. They will feed and you will feel better.

Accept
Accept that others' views are different to yours sometimes. We all have different backgrounds and cultures.

Work

Work to achieve 'win/win' solutions rather than total victory. Very often we want to win arguments at all costs. That is a win/lose situation where you win the argument and the other person loses. A win/win situation is where both parties feel that they have given a little in order to gain agreement.

Live in the present

Live for today rather than the past. Being angry at past outcomes will never bring about future peace.

Look at the situation with empathy.

Understand the other person's point of view even if you disagree with it.

Recognise physical signs of anger

Recognise physical signs of anger such as muscle tension in the neck and stomach. Remember these are signs of stress and anger are parts of the same reaction, the **fight** or flight response. Unclench your fists. Slow your breathing. Get a control of your body.

Be able to take 'time-out'.

Agree to walk away, (flight), rather than allow an intensity of anger to grow, (fight). Agree with the other person that if you feel angry then you will state your need for a 'time out' and that you will walk away for, say, five or ten minutes so that you will get thoughts in order rather than scream or shout or hit.

Ask yourself if your angry outburst will cause happiness or misery.

We all want to be happy. If you say something when you are out of control, you will find misery rather than comfort. Ask yourself if an angry outburst will cause peace or war and act and speak to get happiness. We would all like to cuddle up to our partner this evening rather than be on the settee or, perhaps, be in jail.

Remember the damage
Remember the damage that your anger caused in the past, and think of the happy future that will be built when you have learnt to control your outbursts if it is not too late.

Remember that you have controlled
Remember that you **have** controlled your anger in a wide variety of situations before and then apply those controls to the present situation.

Be concerned
Be concerned with giving and sharing rather than getting your own way. If your anger came from past events, then get your pleasure and happiness today by being in control and getting rid of your rages.

Anger is a dangerous problem because it involves other people and can include violence. This is a very short first-aid section. If you need help then there are anger management specialists who will help you.

Check with your doctor for names.

AFFIRMATIONS FOR CONTROLLING ANGER

I used to be an angry person, but now I control my feelings of rage.

I take slow, deep breaths and allow myself to calm down and regain control.

I am able to see the destructive side of my bad temper and I calm down.

I used to hurt people to show how tough I am, but I am able to control myself and that shows other people that I am strong within myself.

I am calm, confident and in control, now.

I now prefer happiness to anger.

15
WEIGHT CONTROL
PART ONE

BEING OVER OR UNDERWEIGHT CAN HAVE AN INFLUENCE ON SELF-BELIEF. IF IT IRRELEVANT TO YOU, IGNORE THIS PART. IT IS SHARED WITH THOSE WHO WANT TO GAIN CONTROL OF WEIGHT.

PART ONE, THE CAUSES OF WEIGHT PROBLEMS

PEOPLE IN WESTERN SOCIETY are under huge body-image stress. Our ideals of looking good are imposed by movie makers and media superstars. We are bombarded by images of people on television, in films and magazines.

Career progression seems to be related to personal appearance. Fashionable clothes and fashionable body shapes are highly valued, highly prized and often highly priced. People feel that they need to look good to succeed in the giant business corporations of the world.

Children are persuaded to look and act as young adults. They are given role models who are pop-stars and super-models. They are the celebrities who follow the ideas that they need to 'look good' to be successful. Sadly, this usually translates as being thin and sexy. Youngsters attend schools that are the meeting places for youth. They are also crucibles for ideals and criticisms. Unfortunately, they can also be the high-pressure boiler houses where peer pressure and bullying take place.

Set against the huge marketing effort for high energy foods and drinks, items that are often high in sugar and fat, the drive to be thin is enormous and difficult. Those who 'succeed' too well risk eating disorders such as anorexia and bulimia. Those who 'fail' can be seduced into obesity. We have been fed a rich diet of the perfect body shape. But in whose eyes?

Our doctors are best placed to set optimum weights for heights. Actuaries, people who assess life risk factors are able to identify the dangers of smoking and obesity.

Power, sexual and social imaging should be secondary but, unfortunately, short term satisfaction seems to have replaced the need to be healthy.

We have artificially changed our body images by dieting. We have antagonised the systems that have kept us alive for millennia.

Now I will describe a weight and shape control method that really works. The method has nothing to do with dieting or calorie counting. It has nothing to do with fads such as elimination diets, nor eating only protein or carbohydrates or high fibre foods. Those methods can be antagonistic to the natural shape control systems that we have and often end up with the opposite results to those you intended.

Rather than being a new method, this weight and shape control system is as old as humans and other animals. It is something that is built into us from birth. Our own internal resources can be utilised. Until now, we have ignored them. We have failed to recognise the systems that we have. This section will explain how and why your mind and body can work together to help you. It will show you what to do to use them.

The only miracle is the wonder of your bodily processes. The only new thing is finding out how to work with, rather than against, the intrinsic resources that you have. We have been born with the tools we need, but we seem to have lost the handbook. The following is a fresh copy of that manual.

I will show you how to use the psychology and biology of your mind and body to achieve the shape that you want. The methods are safe, easy and effective. Above all, they are natural. They have worked wonderfully well with many people. Be confident that they will also work for you.

We do have body images, blueprints or what are called 'set weights', a biological term used for animals whose weights or shapes do not change. This is the secret of success. Recognising that we do have a sense of shape is the key to a healthier and happier life so please enjoy yours.

Note. Most of the references are made for women. Of the thousands of people that I have helped to lose weight, most have been female. Therefore, I am not being sexist in any way. I am simply making the narrative easier to use. The method works equally well for men.

YOUR BODY-SHAPE-BLUEPRINT

The body-shape blueprint is exactly what it sounds like. Throughout human history our bodies and minds have worked together to establish and maintain the body shapes that optimise our chances of survival. The most variable factor in this body-shaping is the amount of fat that is stored.

Regrettably, the basic shapes that we are given have been corrupted by the abundance of food that exists in modern life and by our attempts to control how we look. We view fat as an enemy that has to be eliminated. Ironically, when we fight our reserves of fat then we encourage our systems to store even more. The battle that we start within our minds and bodies is one that we find difficult, if not impossible, to win.

However, before we progress with the techniques, we need to explore our biology.

Homeostasis
Our bodies are wonderful systems. We maintain balances in many ways. The process is called **homeostasis,** which means 'steady state'. For example, our body temperatures are kept within a very narrow range. We use internal, rather than external, senses to maintain that balance.

We know that on a hot day we sweat. When that sweat evaporates it cools our skin which helps to cool our blood. On a cold one we divert blood from our extremities so that we do not lose heat. If prolonged, this can cause frostbite on our feet and hands. We shiver so that muscular activity warms our blood. These things happen as a response to outside conditions but the outside temperature is only relevant to our internal temperature in terms of what needs to happen in order to maintain our 37°C.

Our homeostatic systems also control the density of our blood, the mix of gases in our blood, blood pressure, sexual drive, sugar levels, thirst, appetite and much more.

Less well known is that our weight, or more exactly our shape, is also maintained within a small range. If we can imagine that we possess a 'blue-print' for shape, then it helps. To use computer terms, we can accept that we possess a 'virtual' thermometer for our temperature, and a virtual chemical laboratory for hormones. To advance the idea of a 'virtual' body-shape-blueprint is reasonable.

Our 'blue-prints' keep our shapes the same, give-or-take a few pounds, until interfered with by life circumstances, social influences and by our attempts to consciously lose weight by starvation methods. Obsessive calorie counting and rapid diets antagonise our well-adjusted systems.

This maintenance of our bodily systems takes place in a small part of the brain called the **hypothalamus**. This brain structure, roughly the size of a walnut, receives sensory information from the body. It then regulates the body to ensure stability.

Metabolism is the name for the chemical reactions that take place in the body that use nutrients to provide energy and to make, or replace, body materials. Metabolism increases during pregnancy, menstruation and the consumption of food. It also speeds up during activity and when there are excess thyroid hormones. It decreases as we get older and during starvation.

The hypothalamus is involved in metabolism. It has affects on levels of hormones such as insulin, thyroxin and leptin. Leptin, from the Greek *leptos* meaning thin, was discovered as recently as 1994 and relates to the fat mass of the body.

161

These hormones, and others, are associated with appetite, weight control and metabolism. They are all involved with fat mass and body weight, something referred to as 'set-weight' for all animals, strangely, with the exception of humans. It is the ideal weight, or shape, for each individual. All creatures have internal body images that are established and regulated. You can watch 100,000 wildebeests run through an African plain and they all look the same. Nobody has interfered with their ideas about fashionable shapes.

Of course, we humans are animals. We also have 'set weights' but I will refer to them as the **body-shape-blueprint** as we need to develop a conscious awareness of our body shapes.

The term, weight, is measured in pounds and kilos. They are artificial concepts that have little relevance to our body shape. To demonstrate this point, if you weigh yourself in pounds, convert that number to stones or kilograms, these new numbers mean very little to you.

Our blueprints have been inherited from our primeval ancestors, but we like to think that we can eradicate our natures with conscious resolve. Our awareness of our shapes is the root of our weight problems. We interfere with our outer appearances to the detriment of our inherent systems. Rather than dieting or calorie counting we need to address our blueprints.

Naturally, different species will have a range of shapes according to seasons and locations. Polar bears put on huge reserves of fat to sustain them through hibernation, but by the time spring appears they are light enough to hunt their prey again. However, their extremes are within a set range. And those variations account for a very changeable habitat.

It is interesting to note that overweight wild animals are rarely seen. This is for three main reasons:

1. First of all, overweight animals are less able to run away from predators.

2. Secondly, underweight animals will be weak and unable to fight off their hunters.

3. Thirdly, and of most relevance to humans, their body blueprints have not been interfered with by concepts of fashion, and therefore remain unchanged. We are aware that domestic animals will become overweight when fed as if they are human.

The first two reasons are linked to survival, and that is the one fundamental purpose of life. We need to survive in our own generation and the next. For hundreds of thousands of years, we have lived among our predators and prey. We have lived in a variety of lands and climates, and still do. Yet we are soft bodied, we lack horns, fangs, claws and scaly armour. How have we stayed alive as a species? The answer is that we are magnificent at surviving and our systems for keeping us alive are perfect.

Yet, tragically, we have an enemy that is all pervading and highly dangerous. It is called civilisation and it threatens us and our offspring. It even endangers our planet. Civilisation is merely a thin veneer over the real animal inside but it has stopped us from hunting for our food. It has tied us to telephones, televisions, desks and computer keyboards.

Stress, anxiety and panic disorders arise from our other main survival system. The 'fight-or-flight' response or the adrenaline rush is one which also causes modern people huge problems. It kicks into action in a world that perceives threats as emotional as well as physical entities. Once more, hormones play a major part in the initiation of this survival reaction. Yet again, at the centre of the response lies the hypothalamus, our little guardian. And there are also very natural ways in which we can mediate the 'fight-or-flight' response when we work with our systems rather than against them.

Before it became excessive, fat WAS good for us

Way back in time, in our cave-dwelling years, humans needed to store fat for the long winters and for when times would be hard. Men needed fat to sustain them during a long and unsuccessful hunting trip. Mothers needed stores of fat in order to survive and suckle their children. Children restricted the time available for mothers to search for food.

Above all, the need to survive famines was paramount. Fifty thousand years ago, life was hard and perilous. Believe it or not, the body's ability to store fat is about survival, and we have been good at surviving as a species until our whole pattern of life was changed by imposed standards of attractiveness, fashion and chic. The natural systems that have kept us alive for hundreds of thousands of years seem to work against us in modern times. That is mostly because we work against them. We are a species that has lived, pretty much unchanged, for hundreds of thousands of years. The great thing is that we are still here. We have survived, and fat is part of that success.

Those primeval roots are still a major part of us. When reference is made to humans as primeval beings, offence is sometimes taken. Rather than meaning that we are primitive, the word means that we have not changed our physiology very much in the last fifty thousand years. That is something that we should be proud of. We got it right back then and we have stayed on this planet to the point where we now dominate every plant, animal and mineral that exists.

If you doubt our primeval natures, consider why we sleep at higher levels than those in which we are awake. Bedrooms usually offer better views of the outside scenery than rooms on the ground floor, yet it seems that we feel the unconscious need to be off the ground to avoid nocturnal predators.

During the warmer months we barbeque our food on an open hearth outside the house. That overcooked, often burnt, food is desirable because it has been cooked as it was in our cave-dwelling days. On vacation we wallow at waterholes (swimming pools) or at the edge of the sea in loincloths (swim-suits). We throw rocks at each other in the shape of Frisbees or balls. Need I go on to make the point?

The key to weight and shape control lies in the recognition of our successful human roots. We are then able to accept an understanding of our blue-prints and our potential to change them.

WHY OUR BLUEPRINTS CHANGE

Throughout history fat has helped to keep us alive. It has acted as insulation. It has been an energy store. It has enabled us to endure famines. It has been our savings account for rainy days. Money has the very much the same purpose that fat used to, but we have retained the need to store fat as well. We can never have too much money but we can have too much fat.

When we look back fifty thousand years to how we were when our unconscious minds and our bodies took responsibility for our well-being, then we can see some startling facts about modern approaches to weight and shape. As with all other mammals, we have the natural capability to fluctuate through the seasons of the year. Other animals acquire stores of fat before winter in order to survive hibernation. We had to do the same, but as we did not hibernate our reserves were regulated within our need to be mobile enough to scavenge during the lean months.

Imagine, for a moment, a woman sitting at the entrance to her cave fifty thousand years ago. Her shape was controlled more by her need to stay alive rather than by any thoughts of health or fashion. She probably gave very little conscious thought to her shape. She had no mirrors, scales or comprehension of her personal weight.

Only in more modern times would external ideals about shape arrive from fashion magazines, films, television and peer pressure. So, way back in time, our cave woman would have been content.

When winter arrived and food became short then she would have relied upon her body fat to remain alive, and if she had children, to keep them alive with her breast milk. She was unable to nip out to the local supermarket to top up her larder.

Had the winter progressed for longer than usual then she would starve. A famine would have begun. If she survived, by the time that food became available again, she would have been very thin.

When food became more plentiful then she would have had the urge to eat to replace the fat she had lost. The crisis would have changed her blueprint to make her larger so that if another food shortage happened, she would be better able to survive. Her fat store was now greater, or in modern terminology, she had become fatter.

Please do not assume that this only applied tens of thousands of years ago. This pattern applied until very recently. We can consider how similar they are to the life-styles in the 19th century for Europeans and for the American settlers. They even apply in the poorer countries of today. In the Western world, food only became very abundant a good few years after the Second World War.

It is this very survival system of storing fat that makes people put on weight after going on a diet. This is at the root of the classic 'yo-yo' dieting process. Our brains, our minds, cannot differentiate between a life-threatening famine and the self-imposed diet. A diet is beyond the remit of the older parts of the brain. The effect of a diet is to evoke an unconscious feeling of danger, the famine response. The biological answer is to increase reserves of fat in order to ensure survival.

Why mothers put on weight
In those early days of human existence people did not have refrigerators or deep-freezers. They had no supermarkets down

the valley. Everything our forebears ate had to be found by themselves. The one safe place in which food would have been stored was in mother. She had the capacity to store food as fat that could be expressed back to the children as breast milk. It is likely that her children would have used her in the same way modern children use a vending machine!

100 years ago, Leonid Brezhnev, the ex-general secretary of the Soviet Union is reported to have been breastfed by his mother to the age of 5 because he was a sickly child and times were hard. Even today there would be no choice for a mother in breast feeding her offspring or have them die from starvation.

Why mothers finish food left on their children's' plates
Mothers seem to have an urge to finish leftover food from their children. Does this strike a chord with you? The vast majority of mothers of young children seem to feel the drive to clear plates, or to cook a little extra when feeding their children. Way back in time there was nowhere to store food for the next day without risk of contamination except in mother. She could then give the stored fat back as milk. Never be revolted, it is a sign of our wonderful heritage.

Why men and women store fat in different bodily locations
When we look back at primeval life-styles, we can see why men and women store fat in different bodily locations. Men as the hunters of larger prey needed extra mobility to escape the other predators and to catch their own food. They would have stored fat on their fronts and backs. It is always strange to see how thin the legs of overweight men are when spotted on a beach.

Women would have been situated more around the homestead in

order to guard their children. They would have foraged and hunted locally. Therefore, women could store fat in a circle around their bodies from the chest to the thighs as they needed less mobility and were the source of milk for their infants.

Why grandparents put on weight

Fifty thousand years ago as men grew older, their sons would have done the hunting. As men aged, they were less able to track animals for the long periods of time that had to be invested. The older men would have grown bigger to have an advantage of power through force. Look at families of gorillas to see how this happens. Men would have localised themselves and would have had a role in the protection and education of their grandchildren. They would have also been at risk when food became scarce.

Until recently, grandmothers tended to put on weight as they grew older. Perhaps in our caves the older women were at the back of the pecking-order after the children, mother, father and her mate if he had survived. She was probably the only female in the family who could not have more children in a crisis. If grandmother had a good store of fat then she was more likely to survive a famine if one happened.

Why we comfort eat

Back in our old family, when the weather started to turn colder then the need to store food as fat would have become greater. The nights becoming longer and the subsequent gloominess made us turn to foods that contained sugars and fats. Call it general anxiety, or the need for greater security, but the drive to consume food grew. If we take the phrase 'comfort eating' and re-name it 'security eating', then the picture becomes clearer. It is the result of the knowledge that winter was drawing closer. They were the times when food became scarcer.

This is why people will lose weight and then regain it quickly after circumstances such as a separation, divorce, bereavement and so on. Fat reserves are then added in case it happens again. This relates to the loss of a hunter/gatherer and it stimulates the need to save fat to last out the future days of possible hardship.

Why overweight people are often fast eaters
Back in time, when we went out and found food growing on bushes or when we had killed an animal, we had two main urges. The first was to consume our bounty straight away because if we went back later then other animals would have eaten what had been left.

The second was to get out of there as quickly as possible before we became prey to the predators that were also hunting for food. So, when we eat quickly, we tend to consume more. The stomach is a very flexible thing that will expand to carry whatever is pushed into it.

When we eat slowly, we put our minds back into the cave where there was little to eat or do. The moral of the story is to slow down when eating. This is the secret of Mediterranean diets where families will enjoy a long, slow main meal at lunchtime rather than rush through a big dinner in the evening.

A modern perspective
The need to survive still exists. We worry about our work, our families, old age, our pensions, health-care, war, terrorism and just about everything. Our civilised ways have not stopped us from having misgivings about life. In our modern lands of

plenty, we store food as fat as if we had to exist for months on our own resources.

Obesity is a contemporary ailment. Rather than using our survival mechanisms to control our weight and shape, we have antagonised our systems by dieting and calorie counting. We strive for the shapes that we are told we should desire with methods that seem to backfire. It is tragic that, until now, we have ignored the tools that we possess already. The successes with the body-shape blueprint method have been achieved by working with the biology and psychology of the human body, rather than evoking a response from dieting which works against the objective of losing weight.

MODERN INFLUENCES THAT CAN CAUSE WEIGHT GAINS

Social influences
People who have been abused may put on weight for protection. Bully victims want to be 'bigger' to avoid physical hurt. We are unable to make ourselves taller, but we can make ourselves wider. Fat may be perceived as armour against punches. Excess fat can also be seen as a repellent of sexual advances.

At the other extreme, the refusal to grow can be an attempt to cling onto childhood, those 'safer' times. This has a bearing on the low-weight problems associated with anorexia and bulimia. These issues are outside the scope of this book and are best helped with specific therapies.

Like father, like son
Size, as in the build and height of a person, is almost certainly to

do with genetics and nurture. However, the amount of fat that is carried by a person is probably more to do with other influences. Overweight people blame genetics as a 'get-out' clause. If a person's parents are overweight, they can blame their ill-fortune on their ancestors and they will be less mentally able to tackle their own size problems.

It might be worth considering that in our survival make-up we might have a predisposition to copy the shapes of those people around us. If they are carrying a lot of fat, then perhaps it indicates that they live in a high risk valley, in primeval terms. Therefore it would seem to make sense that we imitate their shapes to further our own chances of continued existence.

I beg your pardon, but primeval times are over.

We live in times of plenty. As a result of world trading we do not even have seasonal variations in the foodstuffs available every day of the year. Our need to store food is negated by modern methods of refrigeration and farming. If you and your family are overweight, move your minds to the fertile valley in which you already live. The famine will never happen. Stop worrying! Change your blueprint to suit the lush, fertile and abundant valley in which you exist.

In short, lose weight if you are too fat. In current times, this is far more relevant to your survival.

Bigger is worse rather than better

Our culture is based on acquisition. We want bigger houses, cars, bank balances and so on. This desire for more even has a food-orientated description; greed. We live in a commercial society where you can 'buy-one-and-get-one free'. We have offers that encourage us to buy larger portions of 'fries'. We have 'all-you-can-eat' restaurants. And this pushing of food and excessive eating feeds the slimming market.

Think of those offers and promotions as nothing more than an attempt to take your money whilst making you fatter. And when you are fat, there are plenty of people who will take your money by offering diets to help you slim. Remember that fast food is more food, eaten quickly. Bigger is seldom better in terms of health. Being skinny is rarely better either, so starvation diets should be avoided. Rapid results often lead to weight gain. The best solution is to strive to be normal, neither too big, nor too thin.

Bingeing and comfort eating
We have already established that anxiety relates to eating habits such as bingeing and comfort eating. The famine response may be evoked when times seem stressful. Bingeing and comfort eating occur when people feel that hard times are happening, or are coming. If this applies to you, then you know what I mean! Bingeing is similar to primeval feasting. Feasting is a feature within our history. Perhaps finishing food before it went bad, perhaps sharing the outcome of a hunt. They were all to add fat to the personal store in anticipation of 'leaner' days. We still do it in mid-winter to this day, but we call it Christmas or something else.

This leaves nibbling. Nibbling through the day is the way in which other primates consume their food. Those urges are still with us. Very few animals eat a regular set of three meals per day. We do. However, when we combine set meals with nibbling we confuse our systems.

The urge to eat sugar and fat

In primeval days sweet foods were rare. Fruits never seem to have the sweetness of modern confectionary. The fat on wild prey animals tends to be less than modern farmed animals. Older civilisations such as the Kalahari Bushmen will risk life and limb in search of honey. But that is a rare treat rather than something to be found in sweet-shops. In our days of plenty we seem to crave excesses of the foods that were necessary fifty thousand years ago but which are superfluous today.

The mind is a sophisticated thing and is very different to a computer. Logic works in a computer but the human mind runs on emotion as well as logic. We need to make the mind and body feel safe enough to reduce the fat stockpile. In our minds we need to move to that better valley.

FOLLIES OF CALORIE COUNTING AND DIETS

The unconscious systems of the body and mind rank survival higher than a conscious desire to be fashionable. Weight and shape-control are parts of a huge industry. Profit is the goal. Sometimes, this can be at the expense of health. Some industry fat-cats want to convert the dream of weight loss into fat profits.

If just one successful diet had been developed then there would only be one diet that was used by everybody. Has anybody ever got dieting/calorie counting right?

We seem to lack the ability to maintain our shapes in accordance with our conscious desires. Our innate ability to control our body shape is one of the survival systems that have kept us going for all our history, until recently.

174

In order to work WITH the natural systems of the mind and body we must break down some of the main assumptions used in traditional dieting and weight control methodology.

Why calorie counting is counter-productive

The major way in which your body shape is controlled is by metabolism. Some people will burn food at a higher rate than others in order to maintain their blueprint. Other people will burn food at a lower rate.

According to studies into appetite regulation, the daily intake of food is highly variable and correlates poorly with energy usage. Despite this, over long periods of time body weights are usually stable in most adults.

Going back fifty thousand years again, it would have been pointless to burn 1500 calories per day during a famine. Soon the reserves of fat would have been burnt off and our cave dwellers would have died. It is much more likely that in order to hold onto body shape, or reserves of fat, metabolism would have slowed.

In modern times, when a person reduces their calorie intake during a diet, then the metabolism slows to maintain the blueprint shape as much as possible. This is called 'metabolic shift'. This is why dieters will become lethargic and miserable. Their metabolism has slowed to ensure the lowest possible usage of stored energy.

The mind and body are screaming for the things that will replace the fat loss. The best thing to replace lost fat is fat! That is why dieters get cravings for certain products. They are, of course, sugar and fat. And then there is the ultimate mix of the two, chocolate.

We all know people who can eat the whole candy section of a supermarket and remain thin. We also know those who only eat a lettuce leaf and seem to gain a pound. This has more to do with the movement of metabolic rates to maintain the blueprint than calorific intake. When you set your blueprint shape, then you can trust your system to achieve it.

We are different to steam trains! The energy from a certain amount of coal will fuel a boiler for a certain distance. That is measurable. We are humans with a system that works to keep us alive. If we reduce our fuel intake then we will reduce the rate at which we burn it.

Why dieting can be counter-productive
There is a joke about a two page diet book giving a system that should work. On page one it says, 'Eat less, and take more exercise'. On page two it says, 'See page one!'

Reducing food intake only works when it is recognised by the mind and body as beneficial to survival. Therefore, when slow weight reduction at approximately seven pounds per month is translated as a movement towards a beneficial blueprint shape, it is accepted.

When weight loss is rapid it evokes the 'famine-response'. Your system will be driven to add reserves of fat rather than to risk exposure to starvation.

The same applies to elimination diets. We are omnivores. We

eat anything and everything. By doing so, we achieve a balance of nutrients, vitamins and minerals. When we eliminate certain food groups, we signal danger yet again. We are impelled to consume those things that our systems feel we are missing in order to sustain homeostasis.

We are not the only modern species that has become fatter. The animals that we farm are deliberately fattened so that there is more weight per lamb, pig, cow or chicken. This means that there is more fat to be consumed in meat in the twenty-first century than in the many thousands of years ago before farming became driven to produce 'bigger and fatter'.

A wild deer will be leaner because it has to compete for scarce food resources, and as mentioned earlier it would have been at a disadvantage if it were slow in escaping. As farming is an industry, the extra fat that is produced has to be disposed of in the food chain. Those excess fats are found in manufactured foods. It is found in pastries, pies, burgers and savoury snacks. Fats are used to cook foods such as French fries. Fat is added to our food in subtle ways. Not only do we have more food in our times, but we have a higher proportion of fat in our diets.

The same point can be made about sugar. The sources of sweetness in our history were fruits and perhaps, more perilously, honey. Bees want to keep their external stores of sugars.

Now we have used sugar canes and beet to manufacture sugar which is used in our drinks, confections and as an additive to many foods. The high consumption of sugar is contributing to the huge increase in diabetes. The hypothalamus and pancreas have been over-burdened to the point where they are unable to cope.

So, fats and sugars are a danger in excess. Yet fats and sugars are widely used and available. When they are eaten by overweight people they cause 'guilt-trips'. Those feelings of remorse add to anxiety. Anxiety leads to comfort/security eating. That leads to an increase of fat and sugar intake. Additional sugar and fat lead to 'guilt-trips' and so on.

People go on crash diets and count calories in an attempt to slim. The yo-yo dieting cycle kicks in. More weight, more guilt, more food and more fat. The vicious circle is complete. And when obesity and diabetes and heart disease enter onto the scene, the circle is very vicious indeed.

There is a way to break that pattern. We need to look to our history, psychology and biology. We need to use the good sense that we have been given.

16
PART TWO GETTING THE BODY SHAPE YOU WANT.

USING OUR SENSES

We need to address the issues of weight and shape from a different perspective to that of counting calories and fad diets. We need to use the natural resources that we have.

We are able to control our body shapes rather than provoking the responses that work against them. By working **with** our inherent systems, we can encourage weight loss in the medium to longer term.

Although this will seem like a new approach to weight control, it is hundreds of thousands of years old. Only since we started interfering with our natural systems through the use of dieting has the need to regain control of our internal weight and shape mechanisms become of paramount importance.

We are told that we have five senses, namely sight, hearing, touch, smell and taste. They are the ones that we are familiar. They are for becoming aware of the world outside our bodies. They allow us to become acquainted with our environment.

We actually have more than those five. They are the inner senses. They are the ways in which our bodies experience and regulate themselves internally. For example, we have a sense of balance, kinaesthesia. This is the sense that tells you which way-up you are. It is the one that gives you a feeling of movement, direction and orientation when you are in an aircraft.

Then there is another sense that is used in re-setting your body-shape-blueprint. It is called **proprioception**, from **proprius** meaning 'one's own' and per**ception**, which gives you information about where you are in space. It gives you an internal perspective. This is your sense of proportion.

Getting to know what proprioception is.

Please do these exercises. It is important that you become familiar with this sense of bodily feedback. They involve closing your eyes, so please remember the instructions or have somebody read them to you.

Exercise 1.
Extend the first finger on your right hand, extend your arm to the side, close your eyes and then touch the end of your nose with the extended digit.

Which sense did you use to find your nose? You were unable to see it, your eyes were closed. You were unable to taste, smell or hear it. You only felt it when you made contact with your nose.

This is the sense that is used as a preliminary drink-drive test by the American police. It is a sense that is relevant to weight or shape control because it is the awareness of where parts of you are in relation to the rest of you. It is easily switched into.

Exercise 2.
Without moving or touching yourself, feel the sole of your left

foot. You are sending slow nerve impulses to the sole of your foot so that you can verify its existence. Signals are then sent back to tell you that it is there. It is like using radar to detect something and then to pinpoint its location.

Exercise 3.

Again, without moving or actually touching yourself, feel where your right hip is. Now feel where your left hip is. Now feel the space between them. This body checking is going on all the time, but at an unconscious level. However, we can switch our conscious thought into it at will. We can feel our shape within our own mind. This sensory information is being fed into the hypothalamus.

Exercise 4.

When you are ready, close your eyes. Put your hands out in front of you, palm facing palm. Now spread your hands to what you think is the distance between your hips. Then open your eyes and decide how accurate you were. This exercise necessitated you to get proprioceptive feedback and then relay it to your arms and hands. You then verified the position of your hands with an external sense, your vision.

You have now experienced the blending of the two senses that you will use to change your blue-print.

Exercise 5.

Now, with your eyes closed and <u>without</u> touching yourself with your hands, use proprioception to feel the fat on the back of your upper arm as it is. Now feel the shape of that part of your arm as you would like it to be.

This is the insight to weight and shape control. Presume that the feedback goes into a processor, which checks against a blueprint and then changes our system to maintain our shape. This processor is your hypothalamus. Of course, we are unable to see an actual blueprint in a person's brain, but it can be seen within our mind's-eye or, for some people, felt with the mind's hand.

The good news is that we can consciously change our blueprints, and when that is done, our bodies will change their shapes.

Blueprints are re-drawn with visualisation and proprioception. You become aware of every part of your body bit by bit from the shape you are now to the shape that you would like to be, within reason. Within reason is important because the mind and body work for survival. Remember that super-model shapes are for selling clothes, rather than for copying! If you see/feel yourself at an unhealthy body shape, you run the risk of problems.

CHANGING YOUR BLUEPRINT

The first time that you carry out this procedure, go through it slowly. Ensure that you are getting conscious feedback. When this happens, your unconscious blueprint senses are also involved.

Very soon we will embark upon a proprioception awareness routine during which we will start making the changes to your blueprint to achieve the shape that you want to be. However, there is some preliminary work that needs to be done.

COMMENCEMENT DATE:
CURRENT WEIGHT:
TARGET WEIGHT:
DIFFERENCE:
TARGET DATE *:
TARGET DATE 'PICTURE' **

* Calculate your target date by dividing the weight difference by 7 pounds, or 3.2 kilos. This will give you the number of months in which you will achieve your target shape when you follow the instructions given on the recording. Add these months, or part months, to the commencement date to give you your target date.

** Now associate that date with a real point in time. For example, a birthday, anniversary, a holiday or a season. Perhaps something like the appearance of flowers in your garden. Do whatever you can to lock in your target date to an actual point of time.

First of all, write down your current weight in the grid on the next page.

Now write down your realistic target weight.

Work out the difference in pounds or kilograms.

You should aim to lose weight at the rate of 7 pounds, or 3.2 kilos per month. Remember that losing weight at a faster rate runs the risk of evoking the 'famine response'.

LISTS OF FOODS TO AVOID WHEREVER POSSIBLE

On the next page there is a table for you to look at. This includes two lists of the foods that you will avoid until you have achieved your new shape. Rather than being lists of taboo foods, these are highlighted to encourage you to avoid fats and sugars. There will be times when you will be unable to refuse those foods without seeming to be rude. Maybe at a dinner party, for example. However, the fewer of the 'avoidance' foods that you eat, the easier it will be. Remember, in the past you only craved those foods because your mind and body assumed that you were losing fat as part of a famine. Now you are working WITH those systems, so it is very much easier to be free of those old cravings.

In the first column you have 'fatty foods' as a heading. Under that heading there are items such as fried foods. Most people deny that they eat fried foods, but the reality is that they do. Think of a lamb chop being grilled. It is being fried upside down so remove the fat before cooking. Then hard fats such as cheese and butter. Next savoury snacks such as crisps and their many variations that I will avoid naming by brand, savoury snacks and salted nuts. Then hidden fats such as those that are found in sauces, convenience foods, manufactured foods such as pies and take-away foods. Remember fat is cheap and heavy. It is an easy addition to manufactured foods to save costs. Add any other items that you know should be on the list. Read the list and think, item by item, which foods you know you should avoid.

Now in the second column you see the heading 'sweet foods'. There you see items such as cakes, biscuits and cookies, candy and sweets, and, of course, chocolate. Add other items that you know should be on the list. Again, read the list and think, item by item, which foods you know you should avoid.

If you eat other items not mentioned in those lists, or if you drink sugary drinks or you feel that you drink too much alcohol, add these to your list of things to avoid, or limit, under the appropriate headings.

RATHER THAN MAKING THESES FOODS 'TABOO', AVOID THEM WHERE POSSIBLE.	
FATTY FOODS	SWEET FOODS
Fried foods	Cakes
Hard cheeses	Biscuits
Butter	Confectionery
Savoury snacks	Puddings
Hidden fats in sauces, pastries, and fast-food. Manufactured foods such as sausages, pies and pastries.	Chocolate
	Ice cream

Do the proprioception and visualisation exercises given in the next chapter each day for the first three days and then once per week until your new blueprint shape becomes reality.

They are:
1. FEELING AND SEEING YOUR NEW BLUEPRINT SHAPE. This reinforces your new body shape blueprint by communicating with your mind and body.

185

2. SUGGESTIONS FOR CHANGE. Read these through. Say them out loud. They give the positive affirmations that encourage an optimistic outlook.

3. MAKING LISTS OF FOODS TO AVOID WHEREVER POSSIBLE. Although you will find that you almost naturally avoid the foods on your list, it is beneficial to bolster your resolve. Reviewing the lists will give you a feeling of pride in knowing how well you are doing.

THE FOLLOWING ROUTINE needs to be followed once a day for the first three days and then once per week until you have achieved your target shape. The reason is that you are changing a fundamental system that is reluctant to lose reserves of fat that are considered to be important in the primeval scheme of things. It needs gentle persuasion to change. You know that in the past your blueprint would increase easily if your system felt that extra fat reserves would enhance your chances of survival.

FEELING AND SEEING YOUR NEW BLUEPRINT SHAPE

Because you will be quiet and peaceful, it is important that you are in a safe place, free from interruption. If you need to attend to any emergency, you will be instantly alert and wide awake and able to cope.

In the following steps, you will be:

1. 'Feeling' your body shape as it is. (See left sketch.)

2. 'Feeling' where the excess fat is. (Shading in the middle sketch.)

3. Then 'feel' your desired body-shape blueprint as it will be. (Right hand sketch.

The following may be recorded as a script or read. When

recording, miss out the parts in italics. Alternatively, a recording by the author is available from http://www.emp3books.com

Settle down into a really comfortable position and let yourself relax.

The secret of relaxation rests with your breathing. Allow your breathing to expand your stomach rather than your chest. Feel the air flowing gently down into your lower abdomen and then let it flow out smoothly. Avoid inflating the chest. The muscles that pull your rib cage up are for those times when you need a high supply of oxygen in your bloodstream. Switch them off as much as possible. Use your diaphragm instead.

Do that again, feel the air flowing gently down into your lower abdomen...

...and then let it flow out smoothly. The rhythm of breathing will allow you to feel each part of your body with your mind rather than with your hands.

Read the instructions for each part of your body one by one, and then go through the process of sensing it with your mind as it is. Get a good feeling because this is the blueprint that you possess. Remember that the 'feeling' is done with your mind, rather than with your hands. Then feel that part of your body as you would like it to be and as it is going to be.

1. Start with the top of your head; breathe in gently whilst concentrating on the top of your head. In your mind, feel its shape. Now breathe out slowly as if your breath were taking away the excess fat on the top of your head. (In reality, the top

of the head is fairly free of excess fat, but it is a good place to start so that you can work downwards.)

Now breathe into the top of your head, this time sensing it as it will be. As you breathe out, let yourself relax. 'Sense' the new shape for a slow count of five in your mind.

2. Now concentrate on your face. Feel the shape of your cheeks as they are. Feel around the eyes. Now breathe away any excess of fat. Think of your face again. This time, as you want it to be. Sense how it will be; tighter and firmer. The skin now fits closer to the facial muscles. 'Sense' the new shape for a slow count of five in your mind.

3. Now concentrate on your throat and neck as you breathe in. When you have felt your throat and neck as they are, breathe away the fat.

Now feel your throat and neck as they will be. 'Sense' the new shape for a slow count of five in your mind.

4. Now focus on the shape of the tops of your arms, especially the backs where fat covers the triceps. Breathe away the fat. Then feel your upper arms as they will be. 'Sense' the new shape for a slow count of five in your mind.

5. Now feel your chest as it is. In your mind, feel where the excess fat is. Now breathe away the fat. 'Sense' the new shape for a slow count of five in your mind.

6. Now breathe into your upper back. Feel the excess fat. When you have done that, breathe away the fat. Now 'sense' the new shape for a slow count of five in your mind.

7. Be very aware of the shape of your stomach as you breathe in slowly. This is an important area where fat is stored in men and women. Imagine you have the rolls of fat in your hands and you are kneading them like dough. Breathe away the fat. Now sense the feeling of tightness after the fat has gone. Inhale into your

stomach as it will be and experience a sense of pride as you breathe out. 'Sense' the new shape for a slow count of five in your mind.

8. Now grasp the fat on your hips and buttocks with your mind. Do as you did with your stomach. Be aware of the fat dissolving. Breathe it away gently. Feel the taut muscles that were hidden by the fat. 'Sense' the new shape for a slow count of five in your mind.

9. Now feel your thighs. Feel where they are in space, feel where the fat is. Be familiar with those masses of fat and/or cellulite. Now breathe away that fat. The fat has melted away leaving your thighs firm and toned. 'Sense' the new shape for a slow count of five in your mind. Breathe into the shape they will be, feel how much slimmer they are. Feel good.

10. Now your calves. Feel the fat covering the muscle and breathe it away. 'Sense' the new shape for a slow count of five in your mind.

11. Finally your ankles and feet. Feel them as they are and breathe away the fat. 'Sense' the new shape for a slow count of five in your mind.

12. Now sense your whole body as it will be. Sense every part of your body as you want it to be. Breathe in and out slowly and imagine that sense of pride in having achieved your ideal body shape. Breathe in and out slowly again.

13. Now we can combine proprioception with visualisation.

14. *Close your eyes and* Imagine yourself standing in front of a large mirror that reflects every part of you. See yourself naked. See where that excess fat is. Now see that reflection slowly becoming the shape that you will be, the new shape that you felt as you relaxed. Feel good. Feel proud. See the new slimmer and fitter you looking back at you from the mirror.

15. Now place the image of you with that excess fat into the

past. Roll your eyes to your left as you do so.

16. Now place the image of how you will be, into the future. Roll your eyes to your right as you do so.

17. Now create a space in between those images so that you will feel and see the shape that you will be the next time you do these exercises. Then you will feel that real sense of pride at the progress that you are making from the shape you were to the shape that you will be.

SUGGESTIONS FOR CHANGE

Open your mind now to accept the positive and beneficial suggestions that follow.

1. Remember to take time when you are eating. Allow yourself to eat slowly. Enjoy the food; concentrate on the flavour and texture of each mouthful as you slowly chew your food, whether you are alone or with friends and family.

2. Wherever and whenever, sit down at a table and relax while you are eating slowly.

3. When you are choosing food to eat, remember that you have excess fats and sugars in your personal store. What you need to eat are those foods that will give you the vitamins and minerals that your body requires. Allow your body to use that excess fat that you have stored.

4. Know that you will be healthier and fitter when you have used your store of excess fat.

5. Allow your mind and body to work together to achieve your ideal shape.

6. You now find it easy to avoid fats and sugars in foods because your mind is working with your new blueprint to achieve your ideal and healthy body shape.

7. Trust in the ability of your mind and body to direct you away from fats and sugars and towards a healthier way of life.

8. Allow yourself to exercise more. Walk rather than drive, if possible. Take slightly faster steps. Feel the muscles of your body becoming toned and strong.

9. You now find the patience to carry out the 'Seeing and Feeling' exercises in order to strengthen your own sense of body image.

10. You now find the patience for your mind and body to dispose of your excess fat in a healthy way rather than rushing yourself, or by using diets that will promote your 'famine-response'.

11. Hold the image of yourself as you will be in your mind and relax. See yourself in new clothes at your target date. Associate your new body shape with that real point in time. Congratulate yourself on your success.

12. Revert to the pleasures of our ancestors. Savour the sweetness of fruit rather than consuming refined sugars.

In a moment I will ask you to count from 1 to 5 in your mind to yourself. When you reach the number 5, you will wake up; open your eyes, feeling alert and wide awake.

Start counting from 1 to 5 in your own mind…now.

17
QUICK REFERENCE...
Key Points

The negative influences and behaviours from your life can negatively affect your self- belief now and in the future.

Seek balance in your life. Avoid being negatively controlled and avoid controlling others.

Control the amount of control that exists in your life either incoming or outgoing.

Listen more than you talk. People will like you more.

Sharing is a great way to gain happiness and friends. Two or more people in a joint enterprise makes it so much easier.

Love making is sharing whereas sex for one person's relief is hurtful to a relationship.

Look for contentment now and in the future. It is your life, so do what makes you and others happy.

You can train your mind to be positive and you can teach it to stop being miserable.

Believe in your present and future wellbeing.

Eliminate negative thoughts by eliminating negative words in your internal dialogue.

Make positive affirmations about how you want to feel but apply them to the 'here and now'.

Contentment is an emotional thing that never depends on the amount of money that you have. It is free.

Selfish contentment will blow up in your face. Share the joys of life with others.

Think about what you would need to feel really contented and then make that dream a reality by taking positive actions.

Use your imagination to conjure up the emotional results you desire.

Allow the events and people that will help you to achieve your dreams to enter your life and thinking.

A great way to enjoy your thoughts is to take peace from your surroundings and mix them.

Contemplation is a fast way to find relaxation.

Surround yourself with friendly people.

Keep in touch with your friends and family.

Use social media if you find making face to face friends difficult, but be careful when contacting strangers. Some are not what they seem to be.

If you normally do nothing and you are bored and lonely, do something where you can meet like-minded souls.

Being happy is not a sin, it is your right.

Create something that makes you feel a sense of achievement.

Your creations can be for yourself or others.

We all make mistakes but some follow a lack of care and others are from being caring. Be one of the good folk.

Never be dominated. It does not matter who it is, your mother, father, siblings or bosses. Stand your ground. Stop abuse of any type from happening.

Job evaluation happens by bosses. Allow yourself to evaluate how you feel about your work situation. Job satisfaction is vital.

Never let bullies win. The same with predators. They are all weak and puff themselves up to appear bigger than they are. They are more miserable than most.

Be true to yourself. Throw away any masks of deception that you wear.

Become what you want to be by making an effort rather than pretending.

Criticism is destructive.

Praise is motivating and always welcome.

Keeping in touch is easy no matter how far away people are.

Stop people from imposing their presence or views on you.

Avoid imposing your presence or views on other people. Be able to calmly discuss topics.

Transformation is good.

Dump bad memories, cull them.

Look at your problems from own point of view, no blame for others because blame creates anger. Sort out those problems and recycle to good outcomes.

Recall the good things and preserve and keep.

Consider your timescale. Be patient, you will get results in time but you can get them now.

First thing to do to mend a relationship is to stop expecting the other person to change to suit you. That is maybe why there is a bad relationship. You have to mend yourself first then the other person might see you in a different light. You cannot change somebody else, you have to change yourself and then, the other person might just change because they want to.

If you get thrown away it does not mean the end. You still have life and after a bit of sorting and cleaning up then there is still happiness out there.

18

ENCOURAGING WORDS

In short, contentment and happiness depend on sharing and balance. You have the ability to change. Discontent is a frame of mind that can be modified to result on contentment and happiness. All we have to do is make a start.

In your life there will be days when thunderstorms happen. They are short lived and the air clears. Never let an argument simmer in your mind. When the storm has passed return to your calm, contented and happy life.

Stop worrying and start to enjoy the life you have been given. Miracles are few and far between but making positive changes and holding on as tightly as you can to a positive attitude is of paramount importance.

Allow yourself to be happy. Nobody has cursed your life. You are the same as everybody else that has the choice between being miserable and being contented. They made the choice. Rather than following the paths of the unhappy people you meet use the joyful people as role models. Copy their beliefs and style.

Remember, stop worrying and start enjoying your life. Believe in yourself. If you feel your life should improve then make it happen. Your actions, attitudes and words will have been changed by this book. Hold your head high because you are a great person when all the garbage has been removed.

Last words and verbal picture. If at the beginning you were like a car that had been driven through mud, dung and dust that was thrown at it. It looked like a wreck. Now you have taken it through a car wash and it is bright, shiny and polished. Yet, nothing has changed apart from the removal of the stuff that made it look less than it was.

What you see now is the wonderful person you are, and always were under the problems you HAD that hid the real you from others and yourself.

19
A HELPFUL METAPHOR

As an author and a therapist, I love the power that metaphors hold to change the way we think about ourselves. So, as a gift, the following story from my other publications is offered to help you to relax and enjoy the peace while all of the above text is digested by your mind.

RIVER BANK

You're in the countryside, beside a gently flowing small river. A path stretches out in front of you and you're just strolling along.

The sun is beginning to break through the hazy clouds, its warmth becoming noticeable on your forehead. It's comfortable and it's pleasant. There's a stillness in the air, the leaves on the trees hardly moving. The faint scent of the foliage is an agreeable perfume that permeates the atmosphere in a gentle and amiable way.

Birds are singing and chirping; and you can see them sometimes, gliding between the trees and bushes, sometimes hopping from branch to branch.

And by the side of the path you can see grasses and wild plants, enjoying the opportunity to show their green leaves to the sun, absorbing that natural energy, preparing to burst into activity after the long Winter slumber. And here and there flowers are showing themselves to passers-by, to creatures that will help them to create the next generation; to admirers. They almost seem to be boasting to each other. "I'm brighter than you. I'm prettier than you."

The track in front of you meanders with the river, no rush to get anywhere, just taking pleasure from the journey. It seems lazy, but it has its purpose; it will get to its destination, but, in its own time. Within this seeming lethargy, you can sense an energy, a hidden energy which suggests that it's strong but controlled, showing itself only when needed. You can see a large stone in the middle of the stream. The energy shows itself as foaming waves, babbling and chattering, pushing on one side, sucking and pulling on the other.

And you know that over time, the time that it takes, that stone will be smoothed and worn away; it will be dealt with. What was once an obstacle will become just a memory. And as soon as the water has passed that obstacle by, the stream will reform, it will become as it was; still and quiet, peaceful and easy.

In the same fashion, you're aware of the stored vigour in the plants around you, the buds preparing to burst into life, with new leaves, stronger branches, flowers, and seeds.

Meanwhile, the birds are busy making territories and nests; and life itself.

So, you are part of this as an essential element of life, as an observer, and as a participant. It is as if everything that you see, hear, smell, feel and sense is only there because you are there to witness it, as if you are the essential ingredient for the existence of all these things.

But the force of nature that you are experiencing is part of you, your will is as unstoppable as the water in the river, as determined to flourish as every plant that you see, as resolved as every bird you can see and hear, to make your place and destiny. But more so.

You can recognise the potential that you have. It can be used in a conscious way rather than by instinct. You're aware that you can change the way in which you do things.

You know that sometimes that potential is forgotten, sometimes ignored. However it is always there, a store of experiences, some good, some bad; but experiences are the different ways in which new things were done then; the way that you thought the best at the time; and sometimes in hindsight those ways proved to be the best, sometimes those things could have been done in a different way. No matter what you did, you learnt, you gained knowledge that helped, and will help you in future situations.

As you progress along the path, the sun is even warmer and more comfortable, the path smoother and easier to walk and you feel more and more relaxed, more and more at ease with the life you have. You feel more and more confident, that pool of knowledge having become larger and larger.

You see a bench by the side of the river, it looks soft and inviting. A small voice inside your head tells you that you would be lazy to sit here.

The voice tells you to continue, to rush ahead, to get to where you are going in the fastest possible time.

It tells you that anybody who sees you sitting will think you idle, the plants and animals will think you slothful. There is pressure to keep going on, to avoid sitting down. But you want to sit, nevertheless this voice keeps nagging you to go on, to keep pushing yourself. And you're feeling confused.

You decide to sit for a short while, to compromise. As you sit you stare into the water, shapes swirling, changing, depending on where you look, sometimes into the depths, sometimes at the surface. Pictures form and you can see the past and the future. The river always looks the same but it's ever changing.

The water that is passing now has come from the past, but the water that is passing is moving into the future. You can see a vision of what the river will see when it travels on for a while. You can see the path on the bank littered with people who have listened to that voice which condemned them for wanting to rest.

They kept on going, fearful of criticism, fearful of failure. They ignored their own needs, they wanted to reach that place so far away that the closer they got, the further away it would seem to them.

You can see them in that vision, exhausted, stressed, ill and sick. They paid too high a price for their incessant quest for something they could not define, something so abstract like success, recognition or prosperity.

It occurs to you that if the price for those things is too high, perhaps if the goal is wrong, perhaps those people were looking for something that they could have achieved but in a more enjoyable way.

It dawns on you that the real goal is to delight in the path you are on. The river in the future might be wider, it might be deeper, but it will still be the same river. It occurs to you that the plants and the birds will be similar, the sun the same, the bench as soft. But where you are is where those things are, to try to obtain something different by pushing yourself to the point of exhaustion is a pointless exercise.

Enjoy your current path, and then when you are ready, move on at your own pace. The measure of your success lays in the present time, the things that you are doing at this moment. Future gains can be illusory if you ignore the pleasure in your quest for them.

You see a bird overhead, its wings flapping as it gains height, and then it stops and glides for a while before flapping again. The bird will get to where it wants, but with enough energy left to do what it has to do. As your eyes follow the flight of that bird, you see that your destination is very close by, a short cut across a beautiful meadow full of bright yellow and red flowers.

A short cut that would have evaded you had you kept on going intent on following the path. A short cut that did evade those people you saw in your images in the river, those people who were too busy rushing along the path to see where they were going in the longer term.

You stroll lazily across the field, feeling the sun smiling on you, smelling the scent of the flowers, feeling the grasses as they caress your legs. You are content. You are arriving at where you want to be.

Other books by John Smale

Moving Forward

The most perfect thing about humans is our lack of perfection. Moving Forward is the positive outcome of that. We can realise that there is something better in the future. When we berate ourselves for not being perfect, we wallow in failure. But when we see that the future can be better, we thrive in the optimistic feeling that no matter what has befallen us there is always the opportunity for betterment rather than assuming that we have reached an end point. As you read this book either to yourself or to other people you will find insight into problems. This allows movement away from difficulties towards finding solutions and implementing them. The decision to look at life from new perspectives gives the chance to earn your true value in the world and to profit from constructive change. Rather than being held back by old beliefs and attitudes the reader moves into a new way of thinking, a new way of acting and a new way of life. Taking and acting on decisions is paramount to success. By moving forward now, you are investing in a brighter future.

Mind Changing Short Stories and Metaphors

When used in NLP and hypnotherapy, metaphors have long given insights into the difficulties of people and have shown the ways in which we can escape or improve. If the stories strike a chord with you, then they also show a way out. These short stories, metaphors and interactive scripts will help you to eliminate negative thoughts and achieve your dreams by allowing you to relax while reading stories that can bring about positive change. Some of the stories will relax you, others will make you think. Some allow you to enter a light feeling of hypnosis. Hypnotherapy and hypnosis have been major users of metaphors to show different approaches to problems and their resolution. Milton Erickson, the grandfather of modern hypnotherapy used metaphors to great effect in resolving problems with his patients. Self-hypnosis allows you to enter the areas of your mind where you can become imaginative and optimistic. You can create your dreams and the ways in which you will achieve them. Based on a huge amount of therapeutic work, these short stories, metaphors and interactive scripts can help you to bring about positive changes, eliminate negative thoughts and achieve your dreams.

Short Stories and Metaphors

When we look in a mirror we can see a reflection of how we are and how we want to be. We live in a stressful world. Very often we live at a distance from the people who we could ask for help or advice. Regrettably, it is often easier to recognise the causes and effects of problems after the event, with the benefit of hindsight. Therefore, these short stories and metaphors, based on real-life experiences, have been written in order to offer help to people who are suffering, or who might suffer, from negative influences in their lives. The stories are based on the adverse effects that behaviours, attitudes and actions have had on the lives of others. Therefore, if the readers can benefit from recognising symptoms of their own issues that have caused problems, then there is the possibility that they can take corrective action before suffering strikes them. They stem from the therapeutic experiences of a hypnotherapist and how people have exchanged their problems for happiness using short stories and metaphors and NLP.

Hypnotherapy

This is an honest and open book that explains the causes, effects and treatments for many of the problems that a therapist is asked to deal with using hypnosis, hypnotherapy and NLP. John Smale is a therapist who wants to share his many years of experience with existing therapists, new therapists and clients who need to know the truth. It is essential reading for anybody who wants to know more. Owning this book is owning knowledge that will built a therapist's practice because it explains the causes, effects and treatments for many of the problems that a therapist is asked to deal with. Very often therapy is like working on a cryptic crossword. You have to look for clues from your clients. This book helps you by giving a lot of the letters for you to make solving those puzzles simpler. The task of a therapist is to expose the cause of each problem and then defuse the negative effects to build a positive future for the clients. They will trust you to help them. This book makes it easier for you to help them.

FICTION

THE TWISTED SOUL. Part 1 of the TWISTED TRILOGY. A disturbing and mysterious mind-bending story. Dark psychology in a man's journey into his mind and soul

THE TWISTED MIND. Part 2 of the TWISTED TRILOGY. The astonishing and terrifying exposé of a therapist who raped and murdered

THE TWISTED MYTH. Part 3 of the TWISTED TRILOGY. The macabre and mind shocking dark fantasy about the deadly weapon of belief for power.

REVIEW

If you have enjoyed this book and would recommend it to others or if you have any comments, please give a review when asked by amazon or Kindle.

Bearing in mind what has been said about criticism in this book, I would be grateful and very content if you would be kind enough to post a review. Thank you.

CPSIA information can be obtained
at www.ICGtesting.com
Printed in the USA
BVHW041218110819
555506BV00037B/1229/P